Open your Eyes through News in English

Aoi WATANABE
Takayuki ISHII

SANSHUSHA

はしがき

　現代社会は、正に情報の洪水のごとく、毎日様々なニュースが流れる激動の社会と言えるでしょう。その膨大なニュースの中には、非常に興味深く、意義深い情報も見え隠れしています。ニュースはいわば、面白くて奥深い情報の宝庫です。

　本テキストは、流れてくる大量のニュースの中から、興味が持てて、なおかつ、考えさせられる情報を、様々な分野から**14項目を厳選**した、英語で学ぶリーディング教材です。

　本テキストの特徴は、「**話題性**」「**多様性**」、そして「**段階性**」の3つに集約できます。

　「**話題性**」とは、本書が人々の話題に上るニュース記事を取り上げていることです。本書は、現代社会において、極めて重要度が高く、広く関心の的となっている事象を扱っています。「**多様性**」とは、ニュース記事の前後に配置された練習問題やタスクの種類の豊富さを意味します。そして、「**段階性**」とは、章の内外で徐々にレベルを上げるよう意図していることです。各章の記事にレベル（☆印の数で表示）記号を添え、問題やタスクのレベルも意識しています。

　練習問題やタスクは、多様性の理念のもと、段階性を考慮して、3つのセクションに分けて、ニュース記事に添えています。すなわち、**Pre-reading**と**Reading**と**Post-reading**の3段構成になっています。

　Pre-readingでは、写真を見ながら概要説明に触れ、語彙を2段階でチェックし、単語の発音・アクセントにも着目します。

　Readingでは、黙読や音読の練習を取り入れたり、リスニングを合わせてシャドーイングの訓練をしたり、精読を基本とし必要箇所の翻訳に挑戦することも効果的でしょう。本文には注が豊富に用意されているので、読み進めやすいのも特長の1つです。

　Post-readingは、内容把握（「**True/False式問題**」と「**4択問題**」）、文法把握（「**4択問題**」と「**並べ替え問題**」と「**英文和訳**」）、そして発展学習（「**単語チェック＆例文作成**」と「**実践的な会話のリスニングと穴埋め式ディクテーション**」と「**Discussionまたは英作文**」）から成っています。

　更に、**Background of the News Story**と**Practical tips**という2つのコラムにより、各記事の知識を一層深めることができます。これらのコラムと、上記で説明した3部構成を通じて、実に様々な言語活動ができるのが、本テキストの特筆すべき特長と言えるでしょう。

　なお、本テキストは、全体の編集および問題作成を渡邉が、全体の監修を石井が行いました。編集部の山本拓氏には、編集の立場から、有益な提案や助言に加え、暖かい励ましをいただきました。深く御礼申し上げます。

　本テキストにより、英語のリーディング能力を高めつつ、英語力全体の涵養に少しでも役立てることができるなら、編著者・監修者として望外の喜びです。

監修者　石井 隆之

CONTENTS

ニュース英語の構成と特徴 …………………………………………………… 6

第1章 教育・一般① 小学3年からの英語教育 ………………………………………… 11 難度 ☆
Required English from third grade eyed

第2章 テクノロジー① アマゾン Prime Air 発進準備OK？ ………………………… 17 難度 ☆☆
Amazon plans drone delivery of packages in less than 30 minutes

第3章 文化・芸能① "和食"ユネスコ無形文化遺産に ……………………… 23 難度 ☆
Japanese cuisine added to UNESCO intangible heritage list

第4章 海外ニュース① セウォル号の悲劇 …………………………………………… 29 難度 ☆☆
Captain of Sunken South Korean Ferry Arrested by Police

第5章 社会問題① 生殖医療の進歩と前途多難な法整備 ……………………… 35 難度 ☆☆☆
Ruling LDP's debate on family expected to be rocky

第6章 教育・一般② 火山噴火でスヌーピー島出現!? ………………………… 41 難度 ☆☆
Japanese 'Snoopy' island created by volcanic eruption

第7章 テクノロジー② 純国産人工知能ロケットイプシロン、未来に向けて発射！ …… 47 難度 ☆
Launch of the Epsilon rocket

第8章 文化・芸能② 宝塚歌劇団100周年 …………………………………………… 53 難度 ☆☆
A century on stage

第9章 海外ニュース② 謎に包まれたJFK暗殺から半世紀 ………………………… 59 難度 ☆☆
Dallas Observes 50th Anniversary of Kennedy Assassination

第10章 社会問題② スマホの危険から子供を守るには？ ……………………… 65 難度 ☆☆
Parents unaware of dangers faced by children on smartphones

第11章 教育・一般③	コピペにレッドカード ……………………………………… 71 Japanese universities rush to tackle cheating in wake of STAP cell controversy	難度 ☆
第12章 テクノロジー③	近大養殖マグロレストラン ………………………………… 77 'Kindai' bluefin tuna set to delight taste buds in Osaka	難度 ☆
第13章 海外ニュース③	ローマ法王、タイム誌の「今年の人」に ………………… 83 Pope Francis named *Time*'s Person of the Year	難度 ☆☆☆
第14章 社会問題③	Jリーグ初の無観客試合 …………………………………… 89 Soccer: Reds ordered to play behind closed doors for racist banner	難度 ☆☆

ニュース英語の構成と特徴

　母語で新聞を読むとき、ほとんどの人は見出しや写真にざっと目を通して、興味のある記事だけじっくり読み、それ以外は読み飛ばしているのではないでしょうか。ニュース英語を読む場合も、気負う必要はありませんが、いろいろな記事に触れてみましょう。

　英文記事に親しみながら必要な情報を読み取るために、ニュース英語の構成や特徴を把握しておきましょう。ニュースを利用した英語学習の効率がぐんと上がります。

ニュース英語の構成

　限られたスペース内で数多くの情報を伝えなければならない新聞は、一番大切な内容や一番伝えたい要素が、最も目立つようにレイアウトされます。

　まず一番上に、ゴシック体などの大きなフォントで、見出し［headline］が置かれます。号外［extra］が出るような重大事件は、全段大見出し［banner (headline)/ streamer］になる場合もあります。ニュースの"顔"として、具体的かつインパクトのある語彙が使われるのが特徴です。見出しの下に、小見出し［subhead］が来ることもあります。

　その下のニュース本文は、第1パラグラフの書き出し部分［lead：リード］の後に、詳細な説明［body：ボディ］が続く構成が一般的です。

　リードには、発信地と通信社＊の後に、5W（Who, What, Where, When, Why）1H（How）を押さえたニュースの核心が書かれます。この部分でニュース内容の大半を把握できます。続きを読みたくなるような、読み手の関心を引く書き方が工夫されています。

　さらに具体的情報や付随内容を伝えるボディでは、重要な内容が先に述べられ、後に枝葉の情報が続きます。これは、最新ニュースや重大ニュースが飛び込んできた際にボディの最後を削除して、新聞紙面に挿入する必要があるためです。このような形式を、ジャーナリズムでは「逆三角形型［inverted pyramid］」と呼びます。

＊本書では、発信地や通信社等の情報は記事末尾にまとめて記載しています。

見出し [headline] の特徴

● be 動詞の省略

ex) Pope Francis named *Time*'s Person of the Year

　13章の見出しです。通常文として読むと、「フランシス法王がタイム誌の今年の人に名前をつけた」となり、混乱する人もいるかと思いますが、ニュース英語の特徴の一つである、見出しの be 動詞は省略されるという法則を知っていれば即解決ですね。つまり Pope Francis was named *Time*'s Person of the Year（フランシス法王がタイム誌の《今年の人》に指名された）という受動態なのです。

ex) Sony to remain in the red

　こちらも be 動詞を補ってみましょう。Sony is to remain in the red（ソニー、赤字継続の見込み）ですね。見出しの to 不定詞は未来を表すと覚えるのもいいでしょう。will よりも切れ味がいいですね。なお、見出しにおける冠詞はほぼ省略されます。in the red はイディオム表現の「赤字で」なので the が必要です。

●過去の出来事は現在形で

ex) Takashi Yanase, creator of 'Anpanman,' dies at 94

　「アンパンマン」で知られる漫画家のやなせたかしさんの訃報ニュースを扱った見出しです。厳密な時制は has died ですが、英字新聞の見出しでは、新鮮さ、臨場感を出すために、過去や現在完了の出来事に現在形を用います。この法則は第9章の Dallas Observes 50th Anniversary of Kennedy Assassination にも適用されています。

●短い語彙を使用

ex) Required English from third grade eyed
ex) Yahoo and Facebook settle suit, OK tie-up

　一つ目は、英語を小学3年生から必須科目にするという第1章の見出しです。eye という短くインパクトのある語が「目指す」という意味で使われています。二つ目は、ヤフーとフェイスブックが和解交渉に入り提携を承認したことを伝えた記事の見出しです。「承認する」という動詞は approve などですが、それを簡潔に OK という単語に置き換えています。その他にも、「熟考する」を mull、「調印する」を ink のように、シンプルで分かりやすい語が多用されます。動詞以外にも、info(information)、nuke(nuclear)、confab(confabulate)、biz(business)、FY(fiscal year) というように、短い語や略語が好まれる傾向があり、限られた紙面の中で情報を伝える工夫と言えます。

●コンマ、コロン、セミコロン

ex) Yokota's parents, child meet
ex) Mt. Gox files for bankruptcy, hit with lawsuit

　コンマ（,）は、and と置き換えて読みましょう。一つ目は、(Megumi) Yokota's parents and (her) child meet となります。これは拉致被害者の横田めぐみさんのご両親と、めぐみさんの娘の Kim Eun-Gyong さんがモンゴルで面会したことを伝えた見出しです。

二つ目は、ビットコイン取引所、マウントゴックス破綻のニュース見出しです。「マウントゴックスが破産を申し立てて、訴えられる」という意味です。

このようにコンマは、名詞をつなぐ場合にも、節をつなぐ場合にも使えます。

ex) STAP retracted: *NATURE*

コロン（：）は say や according to の情報源や情報の整理に用いられます。「イギリスの科学雑誌『ネイチャー』によると、STAP 細胞は取り消された」となります。

ex) Power use falls; reactors unneeded

見出しが複数の文から成る場合には、セミコロン（；）が使われます。「電力利用が減少。原子炉は必要なし」という意味です。

●アポストロフィやピリオドによる省略や短縮

ex) Gov't ← Government　　　N. Korea ← North Korea

●頭文字［acronym］／愛称

見出しにも本文にもよく使われます。組織名は二度目から省略される場合が多くあります。頻出の省略形や愛称には慣れておくといいでしょう。

ex) DPJ = Democratic Party of Japan　（民主党）
ASDF = Air Self-Defense Force　（航空自衛隊）
IAEA = International Atomic Energy Agency　（国際原子力機関）
WTO = World Trade Organization　（世界貿易機関）
POW = Prisoners Of War　（戦争捕虜）
GOP = Grand Old Party　（米国共和党の愛称）
pinstripes ＝縦縞のシャツ（米ヤンキーズの愛称）

❗ リード［lead］・ボディ［body］の特徴

●時制の不一致

ex) The President told a news conference that it is necessary to ...

主節の動詞が過去形（told）であるにもかかわらず、従属節の動詞は現在形（is）になっています。大統領の発言をなるべくそのまま伝えて臨場感を残すという手法で、ニュース英語によく見られます。

●客観性を保つ語彙や表現

reportedly や allegedly などは中立を保つ際に頻出する副詞です。また The company is expected to ... や It is estimated that ... といった受動態も頻繁に使われます。こうした副詞や受身形は、断定を避けたり、ニュースのトーンを和らげたり、客観性を持たせたりする効果があります。

以下も、客観性を保つために工夫されたニュース英語特有の表現例です。

ex) Police quoted the suspect as saying that ...

直訳すると「警察は容疑者が…と言っていると引用している」ですが、つまり「警察によると、容疑者は…と言っている」という意味です。the suspect を主語にして、The suspect is quoted as saying that ... のように「警察」を省略してしまうパターンもあります。

●分詞構文

　　ex)　Powerful Tsunami occurred, killing at least 30 people.

　「強い津波が起きて、少なくとも 30 名が亡くなった」の意味ですが、津波発生の事実と、その結果の被害状況について簡潔に述べています。このような分詞構文も、ニュース英語で多用される表現です。

●書き方における自由な発想

　文法が単純で、内容を重視するニュース英語は、自由な発想もその特徴といえるでしょう。たとえばニュース英語では、同じ語の繰り返しを避け、言い換えを重ねる中で情報が追加されることがよくあります。定番の言い換え例としては、「国連（the United Nations）」→ World Body、「内閣官房長官（Chief Cabinet Secretary）」→ Prime Minister's right hand man などがあります。

　首都を「政府」の意味で使うことも、ニュース英語の特徴の一つです。Tokyo and Washington は「日本政府と米政府」を表します。

　また、従来と異なる使い方が定着することもあります。たとえば、少し前までは euthanasia（安楽死）は名詞で、euthanize（安楽死させる）という動詞はありませんでしたが、今では辞書にも載っています。

　その他、ダッシュ（―）を利用した説明の挿入や、単語を組み合わせた群形容詞もよく使われます。murder-for-insurance case（保険金殺人事件）、hit-and-run（ひき逃げの）などの例がありますが、これらは長文にしないための工夫の一つであり、ニュース英語の特徴といえるでしょう。

ニュース英語を学ぶみなさんへ

　英語とニュースを同時に学ぶことができる News in English は、貴重な情報の宝庫です。グローバル化の波が世界中に届く現代社会の、未来の担い手となる学生のみなさんが利用しない手はありません。「ニュース英語の構成と特徴」では、ニュース英語を効率的に教材として活用するコツをお伝えしました。様々なニュースに触れ、eye-opening な気づきのきっかけとなればそれに勝る喜びはありません。

　また同時に、忘れないでいただきたいことは、「形になってメディアに登場するニュースよりも、形にならないまま忘れ去られるニュースのほうがずっと多い」ということです。新聞やテレビやネット上で取り上げられ、多くの人々の目に触れるニュースは、政治的な都合や世間の注目度に左右されて表に出ます。同じニュースであっても、報道機関や国籍により切り口や表現はまったく異なります。ひとつのニュースに出会ったとき、そのニュース報道を鵜呑みにしたり、踊らされたりするのではなく、表舞台に出てこないストーリーにも思いを馳せ、常に想像力を働かせ、地球規模で多角的に物事を考える人になってください。

　ニュース英語は、英語力を向上させ、国内外の情報を収集できるすばらしい教材です。どんなジャンルのニュースでも構いません。興味を持ったニュースから始めて、皆さんの世界を拓いていってください。

　監修の石井隆之先生、英語校閲の Wade Cruz 先生、翻訳協力の尼崎江奈さん、三修社の山本拓さんに心より感謝申し上げます。

渡邉 あをい

■写真提供

p.11: ©iStockphoto.com/CEFutcher
p.17: ©AFP＝時事
p.23: ©iStockphoto.com/runin
p.29: © 読売新聞社
p.35: ©iStockphoto.com/skynesher
p.41: © 朝日新聞社
p.47: © 読売新聞社
p.53: © 時事
p.59: ©Photoshot/ 時事通信フォト
p.65: ©iStockphoto.com/Jodi Jacobson
p.71: © 株式会社アンク
p.77: © 近畿大学水産研究所
p.83: ©iStockphoto.com/neneos
p.89: © 時事

教育・一般①

第1章：小学3年からの英語教育

単語数：588
難度 ★☆☆

Before Reading

　「グローバル化」という言葉が定着して久しいが、日本人の英語レベルは決して高い位置にはない。東京五輪開催の2020年にはスタートする小学3年生からの英語教育。実りある授業にするための、教育内容と指導方法の徹底的な検証と入念な準備が必須だ。

◼ Basic Vocabulary Building

英語に合う日本語を選びましょう。

1. concrete □
2. ministry □
3. accustomed □
4. specialized □
5. reform □

a. 省
b. 専門の
c. 改革
d. 具体的な
e. 慣れた

◼ Advanced Vocabulary Building

英語に合う日本語を選びましょう。

1. full-fledged □
2. obligatory □
3. boost □
4. considerably □
5. human resources □

a. 相当に
b. 人材
c. 本格的な
d. 増加させる
e. 必須の

◼ Pronunciation Training

アクセントのある母音に○をつけ、発音に注意して5回声に出して読んでみましょう。

1. current　2. elementary　3. verbal　4. recommendation　5. emphasis

11

Let's Read

Required English from third grade eyed

The education ministry is considering moving up the starting year of obligatory English-language education in elementary schools to the third grade from the current fifth grade by around 2020, government officials said Wednesday.

5 The move would force the government to considerably boost the number and quality of English teachers and native-language assistant teachers at more than 22,000 six-year elementary schools with 7.1 million children across the country.

During his daily press briefing, Chief Cabinet Secretary Yoshihide 10 Suga said children should be given more English lessons and at an earlier age in elementary school.

"(The government) will consider concrete (education reforms), including moving up the starting year from the current fifth," Suga said.

The education ministry came up with the idea in response to a 15 government education panel's call for developing human resources needed in this age of globalization. The idea was included in the panel's policy recommendation report published in May.

Under the current system, a 45-minute English lesson is held once a week for fifth- and sixth-graders in elementary school.

20 Currently the emphasis is on getting children accustomed to the English language through simple verbal communication, such as singing songs and playing games, rather than teaching grammar and reading and writing skills.

The education ministry is now considering upgrading the lessons for 25 fifth- and sixth-graders to full-fledged language classes, including written English, a ministry official told *The Japan Times*, noting these classes might take place three times a week.

Right now, about 10,000 native speakers are working as assistant language teachers (ALTs) at elementary, junior high and high schools 30 across the country.

If the reform plan is formally adopted by the central education panel under the government, the education ministry would probably boost the number of ALTs, the official said.

Some experts, however, expressed concern over the government plan.
35 Goro Tajiri, a professor at Kansai University in Osaka, said teachers in elementary schools are in no way prepared for such a program.

NOTES

eye 視野に入れる
ministry 省
obligatory 義務的な、必須の
current 現在の

considerably かなり、相当に
boost 増加させる

concrete 具体的な

come up with ～を考え付く
in response to ～に応えて
human resources 人的資源、人材
globalization グローバル化
emphasis 強調、重要視
accustomed to ～に慣れる
verbal 言葉の

full-fledged 本格的な

in no way 少しも～ではない

"I don't think (the plan) is a good idea. (Schools) are not ready at all," said Tajiri, a noted expert on English education who often observes English lessons in elementary schools.

Tajiri said most teachers handling English lessons in elementary schools have not had specialized language-teaching training, and some end up teaching incorrect pronunciation and grammar.

With just seven years until 2020, there wouldn't be enough time to retrain them or develop good English-teaching materials for them to use, Tajiri warned.

He said that to develop human resources that can help Japan in the age of globalization, what really counts and needs reforming is English education in high schools and universities, as elementary school teachers, after all, can only teach simple conversational phrases.

【Oct 23, 2013 | Japan Times】

NOTES

specialized 専門の

end up ~ing（結局）
〜に終わる

retrain 再教育する

BACKGROUND OF THE NEWS STORY

　小学校における英語教育は、文部科学省の「英語が使える日本人の育成のための行動計画」（2003年3月）を元に、文科省指定の研究開発学校（国立大学付属小学校と構造改革特別地域内の小学校）で先行実施され、その実施状況を踏まえて2008年度から小学5、6年生を対象に始まった。2011年度には必修化されたが、道徳や総合学習と同様に正式な教科ではない。その開始時期を前倒しして小学3年生からとする方針が固まった。

　3、4年は週1〜2回、クラス担任とALT（ネイティブの指導助手）が、英語コミュニケーションを通じ、英語に触れて親しむ機会を提供する。小学5年生からは教科に格上げし、週に3回程度教科書を使用して基本的な読み書きなど、中学校の学習内容を一部取り入れ、成績評価も導入される。早い時期から基礎的な英語力を身に付ける機会を設け、国際的に活躍できる人材育成につなげる狙いだが、日本語教育優先を求める声や、成績評価は英語嫌いを招くといった意見もあり足並みは揃わない。教員の指導力向上、授業時間の確保等、実現に向けての課題が山積している。

Comprehension Check

◘ *True or False*

英文を日本語にし、ニュースの内容に合っていればT（True）、間違っていればF（False）に〇をつけましょう。

1. English education at present starts from fourth grade.

   (T ／ F)

2. The schools are ready for teaching English earlier than the present system.

   (T ／ F)

3. Once the program is implemented, the government will need more Assistant Language Teachers.

   (T ／ F)

◘ *Multiple Choice*

適切なものを（A）（B）（C）（D）より選びましょう。

1. What's the word that we can't use to replace "obligatory"?
   (A) compulsory　(B) mandatory　(C) required　(D) voluntary

2. One of the ＿＿＿＿＿＿＿ for the program stresses that reforming English education in high schools and universities is needed much more than in elementary level.
   (A) supporters　(B) opponents
   (C) advocates　(D) proponents

3. The idea of earlier English education is to deal with the age of ＿＿＿＿＿＿＿.
   (A) globalization　(B) militarization
   (C) innovation　(D) feudalization

Practical Tips

- 文部科学省の英語正式名はMinistry of Education, Culture, Sports, Science and Technologyとてんこ盛りです。今回のニュース記事ではthe education ministryとあるように、英語ニュースでは伝える内容に関連する産業のみを小文字で表す場合が多いです。ちなみに大臣はministerです。
- 必須にあたる英語はrequired, obligatory, compulsoryのほか、mandatoryなどもあります。Multiple Choice1番の大きなヒントですよ！
- 見出しのRequired English from third grade eyed「小学3年からの英語教育」については本書冒頭の「ニュース英語の構成と特徴」もご参照ください。

Grammar Build-up

■ Incomplete Sentence

適切なものを（A）（B）（C）（D）より選び、文法上正しい英文を完成させましょう。

1. The couple are considering _____ to a rural area from urban.
   (A) move　(B) moving　(C) to moving　(D) to move

2. The President made an apology _____ the public outcry.
   (A) for the sake of　(B) in order to
   (C) in response to　(D) in spite of

3. Annie has _____ a good idea to solve the problem.
   (A) given rise to　(B) come up with
   (C) got along with　(D) made up of

■ Rearrange in the Correct Order

順番を並べ替えて、意味の通る英文にしてください。（最初の文字は大文字に変更してください。）また、それを日本語にしましょう。

1. examples ／ some ／ me ／ give ／ concrete ／ please
   英文：＿＿＿＿＿＿＿＿＿＿＿＿＿＿＿＿＿＿＿＿＿＿＿＿
   訳：＿＿＿＿＿＿＿＿＿＿＿＿＿＿＿＿＿＿＿＿＿＿＿＿

2. makeup ／ up ／ ended ／ examinations ／ taking ／ I
   英文：＿＿＿＿＿＿＿＿＿＿＿＿＿＿＿＿＿＿＿＿＿＿＿＿
   訳：＿＿＿＿＿＿＿＿＿＿＿＿＿＿＿＿＿＿＿＿＿＿＿＿

3. accustomed ／ game ／ using ／ he ／ consoles ／ to ／ is
   英文：＿＿＿＿＿＿＿＿＿＿＿＿＿＿＿＿＿＿＿＿＿＿＿＿
   訳：＿＿＿＿＿＿＿＿＿＿＿＿＿＿＿＿＿＿＿＿＿＿＿＿

■ English-Japanese translation

次の英文の動詞を○で囲み、日本語にしましょう。

1. Japan finally decided to participate in the full-fledged negotiation on TPP.

2. More than 80% of domestic violence victims surveyed say that they in no way regret their choices to leave their homes.

3. The human resources department has received more applications for voluntary retirement than expected.

Further Study

◘ *Make sentences using the following words*

下の英単語の、ニュース本文の中で使われている品詞と意味を辞書で調べて書き、その単語が入った8ワード以上のオリジナルセンテンスを作りましょう。

	品詞	意味	その他の品詞や意味
1. emphasis	____	_____	_____
2. accustomed to	____	_____	_____
3. verbal	____	_____	_____

◘ *Speak up about the News*

以下の会話を聴き、空欄を埋めましょう。

Jijio: I received the (　　　) of my previous TOEIC exam. It's lower than I (　　　). I feel a bit sad.

Newcy: Oh, I'm sorry to hear that but if you (　　　) taking exams, I think it will be improved.

Jijio: I hope so. Would you like to (　　　) (　　　) (　　　) (　　　)?

Newcy: Hmm, maybe someday. Wait. I heard about news that the government is planning to (　　　) English education. It is going to start from 3rd grade from the (　　　) 5th grade. What do you think?

Jijio: I envy them. Earlier is better especially (　　　) (　　　) (　　　) (　　　) listening comprehension skill. It will help (　　　) them globally competitive in the future.

Newcy: Well, maybe so. However, I think we shouldn't forget our (　　　) (　　　), because it is part of our (　　　).

◘ *Voice your Opinion*

What is your definition of "globalization"?
What do you think is the most important in order to raise global-minded people?

テクノロジー①

第2章：アマゾン Prime Air 発進準備 OK ?

単語数：464
難度 ★★☆

Before Reading

　ネットで注文してから30分後には、小型無人飛行機が商品をあなたの手元に届けてくれる！　SF映画の1シーンのような近未来型配達システムが今、実現に向けて動き出そうとしている。

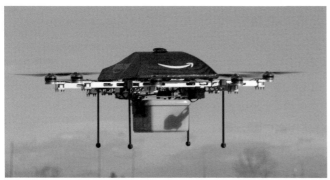

■ Basic Vocabulary Building

英語に合う日本語を選びましょう。

1. civilian
2. avoidance
3. prime
4. standpoint
5. unmanned

a. 回避
b. 民間の
c. 観点
d. 無人の
e. 最上の

■ Advanced Vocabulary Building

英語に合う日本語を選びましょう。

1. pesticide
2. speculate
3. outstanding
4. aviation
5. collision

a. 傑出した
b. 衝突
c. 航空（学）、飛行（術）
d. 殺虫剤
e. 推測する

■ Pronunciation Training

アクセントのある母音に○をつけ、発音に注意して5回声に出して読んでみましょう。

1. package　　2. vehicle　　3. priority　　4. pesticide　　5. urban

Let's Read

Amazon plans drone delivery of packages in less than 30 minutes

New York — Amazon.com is working on a way to get packages to customers in 30 minutes or less — by drone.

Consider it the modern version of a pizza delivery boy, minus the boy. Amazon.com said it's working on the so-called Prime Air unmanned aircraft project in its research and development labs. But the company says it will take years to advance the technology and for the Federal Aviation Administration to create the necessary rules and regulations.

The project was first reported Sunday by CBS' "60 Minutes."

Amazon CEO Jeff Bezos said in a prime-time interview that while the octocopters look like something out of science fiction, there's no reason they can't be used as delivery vehicles.

Bezos said the drones can carry packages that weigh up to five pounds, which covers about 86 percent of the items Amazon delivers. The current generation of drones the company is testing has a range of about 16 kilometres, which Bezos noted could cover a significant portion of the population in urban areas.

While it's tough to say exactly how long it could take the project to get off the ground, Bezos told "60 Minutes" that he thinks it could happen in four or five years.

One of the biggest promises for civilian drone use has been in agriculture.

The unmanned aircraft can fly over large fields and search out bugs, rodents and other animals that might harm crops. Then, thanks to GPS, another drone could come back and spread pesticide on that small quadrant of the field.

Agriculture is also seen as the most-promising use because of the industry's largely unpopulated, wide open spaces. Delivering Amazon packages in mid-town Manhattan will be much trickier.

Besides regulatory approval, Amazon's biggest challenge will be to develop a collision avoidance system, said Darryl Jenkins, a consultant who has given up on the commercial airline industry and now focuses on drones.

Who is to blame, Jenkins asked, if the drone hits a bird, crashes into a building? Who is going to insure the deliveries?

There are also technical questions. Who will recharge the drone

---

NOTES

drone 無人機

unmanned 無人の

Federal Aviation Administration（米国）連邦航空局
regulation 規制
prime-time ゴールデンタイムの

current 現在の
range 範囲
significant portion かなりの部分

get ～ off the ground ～を順調にスタートする

civilian 民間の

bug 虫
rodents 齧歯（げっし）動物
crop 作物、収穫物
GPS = Global Positioning System 全地球測位システム
quadrant 4分の1の区域
promising 前途有望な
tricky 扱いにくい
besides ～ ～のほかに
regulatory 規制の
approval 認可
collision 衝突
avoidance 回避
give up on ～に見切りをつける

batteries? How many deliveries can the machines make before needing service?

"Jeff Bezos might be the single person in the universe who could make something like this happen," Jenkins said. "For what it's worth, this is a guy who's totally changed retailing."

The biggest losers could be package delivery services like the U.S. Postal Service, FedEx and UPS.

FedEx spokesman Jess Bunn said in an email: "While we can't speculate about this particular technology, I can say that making every customer experience outstanding is our priority, and anything we do from a technology standpoint will be with that in mind."

【Dec 3, 2013 | By Scott Mayerowitz — AP】

NOTES

crash 衝突する
insure 保証する
universe 宇宙
for what it's worth 価値があるかわかりませんが、あくまでも私の意見ですが
retailing 小売業

speculate 推測する
outstanding 傑出した
priority 優先順位
standpoint 見地

BACKGROUND OF THE NEWS STORY

　アマゾン創業者でCEOのジェフ・ベゾス氏が、CBSのドキュメンタリー番組「60ミニッツ」で、オクトコプター（モーターで駆動する8つの翼があり胴体の下部に商品を入れるバスケットが付いているマルチコプター）によるデリバリーサービス「プライム・エアー」の開発を明らかにした。
　軍事利用で普及した無人機ドローンは、機器の価格低下に伴い、商業用の可能性が広がっている。アマゾン以外にも、ドミノピザが「ドミノコプター」によるピザ宅配を計画中だ。アメリカ連邦航空局（Federal Aviation Administration）が小型無人機の商業利用解禁に踏み切れば、ビジネスとして有望視される小型無人機関連事業への投資額は、2013年前年同期の2倍に当たるおよそ4090万ドル（およそ40億円）に急増する。2020年には、官民合わせて3万の無人機がアメリカを飛行し、無人機は900億ドル規模の産業に成長し、10万人の雇用を生むという試算もある。ただ、"technology has always been a double edged sword."（技術は常に諸刃の剣）であり、「プライム・エアー」の大都市マンション地域での利用は厳しそうだ。

Comprehension Check

◼ *True or False*

英文を日本語にし、ニュースの内容に合っていればT（True）、間違っていればF（False）に○をつけましょう。

1. Amazon. com's aerial delivery system is so popular among customers that a majority of them are now using the service.
   (T ／ F)

2. The mini aircraft is capable of carrying up to five pounds of goods.
   (T ／ F)

3. Some carriers are preparing to file a complaint against Amazon. com.
   (T ／ F)

◼ *Multiple Choice*

適切なものを（A）（B）（C）（D）より選びましょう。

1. _____ is responsible for making rules and regulations of commercial drones.
   (A) NSA (B) NASA (C) FDA (D) FAA

2. The CEO of Amazon.com unveiled its Prime Air _____.
   (A) at a press conference (B) on a TV program
   (C) in a tech show (D) on the radio

3. The unmanned aircraft is highly likely to be used _____.
   (A) in mid-town Manhattan (B) on a stock market
   (C) in large fields (D) in the universe

Practical Tips

- 今回は「無人」の乗り物unmanned vehicleという表現が出てきます。manは「（乗り物などに）人員を配置する」という動詞です。manned space flightになると「有人宇宙飛行」です。日本語で同じ「無人」であっても「無人島」であれば、uninhabited islandで、「無人踏切」であれば、unattended crossingとなります。
- ニュースの中で「衝突」に当たる英語は、crashとcollisionが出てきます。crashは、動いている物が止まっている物などにぶつかるという場合に使います。飛行機の墜落事故には必ずといっていいほどcrashが使われています。collision（動詞はcollide）は、動いている物同士の衝突に使われます。head-on collisionは「正面衝突」のことです。

Grammar Build-up

Incomplete Sentence

適切なものを（A）（B）（C）（D）より選び、文法上正しい英文を完成させましょう。

1. The GPS _____ Global Positioning System.
   (A) stands for　(B) stays away　(C) starts with　(D) singles out

2. He is the _____ person to tell a lie.
   (A) most　(B) least　(C) last　(D) best

3. The scientists are trying to get the research _____ the ground.
   (A) on　(B) off　(C) with　(D) for

Rearrange in the Correct Order

順番を並べ替えて、意味の通る英文にしてください。（最初の文字は大文字に変更してください。）また、それを日本語にしましょう。

1. blame ／ to ／ partly ／ the ／ media ／ is

   英文：_____

   訳：_____

2. happy ／ businesspersons ／ good ／ customers ／ make ／ must

   英文：_____

   訳：_____

3. reason ／ cry ／ there ／ no ／ to ／ is

   英文：_____

   訳：_____

English-Japanese translation

次の英文の動詞を○で囲み、日本語にしましょう。

1. Some pesticides can be harmful for humans and animals.

   _____

2. The United States was found to have bugged communications of some world leaders.

   _____

3. The meeting droned on all day long.

   _____

Further Study

■ Make sentences using the following words

下の英単語の、ニュース本文の中で使われている品詞と意味を辞書で調べて書き、その単語が入った8ワード以上のオリジナルセンテンスを作りましょう。

	品詞	意味	その他の品詞や意味
1. range	_____	_____	_____
2. promising	_____	_____	_____
3. tricky	_____	_____	_____

■ Speak up about the News

以下の会話を聴き、空欄を埋めましょう。

Jijio: Oh! I forgot to buy the book that I need for my thesis. I need it (　　　　) (　　　　). I hope the book will fly directly to me.

Newcy: Do you know about the new delivery system Amazon (　　　　) (　　　) (　　　　)?

Jijio: I have heard about it but I think it's ridiculous. I think it's impossible to clear many hurdles.

Newcy: Yeah, maybe it'll take some time but I admire the frontier (　　　) of Jeff Bezos. I think he is (　　　) of the best entrepreneurs in the tech (　　　).

Jijio: I (　　　) with you in that respect. At least the new technology is more (　　　) than driving trucks around. Oh, I wish I could use the service right now!

■ English Composition

次の日本語を英語にしましょう。

1. そのプロジェクトを完成させるためには数か月はかかるだろう。　**take を使って**

   _____

2. Miho は人口の多い都市から人口の少ない田舎に引っ越しをした。
   densely-populated urban area と sparsely-populated rural area を使って

   _____

3. 車の衝突事故で5名が軽傷を負った。　**head-on collision を使って**

   _____

文化：芸能①

第3章："和食" ユネスコ無形文化遺産に

単語数：468
難度 ★☆☆

Before Reading

　四季や変化に富む地形がもたらす「新鮮で多様な食材」「自然の美しさを表現した盛り付け」の「和食」が「日本人の伝統的な食文化」として認められた。会席料理だけではなく、庶民が毎日口にする和食もまた対象だ。世界の和食ブームに火がつくだろうか？

◼ Basic Vocabulary Building

英語に合う日本語を選びましょう。

1. appreciate　　　　　　a. 引き金となる
2. asset　　　　　　　　b. 正しく理解する
3. intake　　　　　　　 c. 摂取（量）
4. trigger　　　　　　　d. 料理
5. cuisine　　　　　　　e. 財産

◼ Advanced Vocabulary Building

英語に合う日本語を選びましょう。

1. heritage　　　　　　 a. 多様性
2. diversity　　　　　　 b. 無形の
3. intangible　　　　　　c. 連帯
4. sufficiency　　　　　 d. 遺産
5. solidarity　　　　　　e. 十分

◼ Pronunciation Training

アクセントのある母音に○をつけ、発音に注意して5回声に出して読んでみましょう。

1. cuisine　　2. recognition　　3. ancient　　4. enhance　　5. benefit

Let's Read

Japanese cuisine added to UNESCO intangible heritage list

"Washoku" traditional Japanese cuisine was added to UNESCO's Intangible Cultural Heritage list Wednesday, raising the government's hopes of enhancing its global recognition, attracting more foreign tourists and boosting exports of the country's agricultural products.

The Japanese government's proposal was formally approved by the U.N. Educational, Scientific and Cultural Organization at a meeting of its Intergovernmental Committee in Baku, Azerbaijan. Japan's cultural affairs agency said, adding that the panel valued the spiritual tradition of respecting nature associated with washoku.

The move comes as the country faces a low food self-sufficiency rate of around 40 percent on a calorific intake basis as well as the spread of Western eating habits. Washoku became the 22nd Japanese asset to be listed on UNESCO's Intangible Cultural Heritage list, which also includes Kabuki, Noh and Bunraku.

"We are truly happy," Prime Minister Shinzo Abe said of the UNESCO recognition in a statement released early Thursday morning. "We would like to continue passing on Japanese food culture to the generations to come... and would also like to work harder to let people overseas appreciate the benefits of washoku."

The Japanese government is hoping that the registration will help ease safety concerns over the country's food products following the Fukushima nuclear disaster triggered by the March 2011 earthquake and tsunami.

As changes in social and economic structures as well as the globalization of food have raised concern about whether communities can continue to pass down traditional Japanese dietary cultures, the government also hopes the heritage listing will help the younger generation to recognize the value of such cultures.

Kiyotoshi Tamura, an official of the Organization to Promote Japanese Restaurants Abroad, expressed hopes that efforts will be made to advertise Japanese foods, saying, "The recognition of Japanese cuisine will definitely increase. I hope people around the world will familiarize themselves and promote it."

The government made a proposal for UNESCO registration of the country's food culture in 2012, backing a campaign initially launched by the Japanese Culinary Academy, a nonprofit organization made up of chefs in the ancient Japanese capital of Kyoto and other parts of Japan.

In its proposal, "Washoku: Traditional dietary cultures of the Japanese," the government said Japanese food across the country has basic common characteristics but also has "great diversity" based on geography and history, leading to the use of various kinds of seafood and agricultural products.

It also said Japanese food has developed as part of daily life, has a strong connection to seasonal events such as the celebration of New Year and is constantly recreated in response to changes in the natural and social environments.

In October, the UNESCO body recommended Japanese food be recognized as intangible cultural heritage, saying it plays a major role in social solidarity.

UNESCO had previously registered four food cultures — French cuisine, traditional Mexican food, the Mediterranean diet in countries such as Spain and Italy, and "keskek," a Turkish ceremonial dish — as such assets.

【Dec 3, 2013 | Kyodo】

BACKGROUND OF THE NEWS STORY

　国際連合教育科学文化機関（United Nations Educational, Scientific and Cultural Organization = UNESCO）の遺産事業には、有形の貴重な建築物、遺跡や環境を対象とする「世界遺産（World Heritage）」、歴史的に貴重な文書や絵画、楽譜、映画などの記録物を対象とする「世界記憶遺産（Memory of the World）」、芸能や伝統工芸技術、社会的慣習を対象とする「無形文化遺産（Intangible cultural Heritage）」がある。食文化では、和食の他、フランスの美食術、メキシコの伝統料理、韓国のキムチ文化、トルコのコーヒー文化なども登録されている。

　当初はプロが作る会席料理の登録を想定していたが、庶民が日々口にする料理も含め推薦された。文化庁は、日本食文化は日本人が基礎としている「自然の尊重」という精神にのっとり、正月や田植え、収穫祭のような年中行事と密接に関係し、家族や地域の人との結びつきを強める社会習慣であるとしている。登録は東日本大震災後の原発事故により風評被害を受けている日本食に対する信頼を回復し、復興のシンボルとして世界に向けてアピールする絶好の機会ともなろう。

Comprehension Check

■ True or False

英文を日本語にし、ニュースの内容に合っていればT（True）、間違っていればF（False）に〇をつけましょう。

1. The proposal to register Washoku as UNESCO's list was made almost a decade ago.

   (T ／ F)

2. Japan's self-sufficiency ratio is well over 50 percent.

   (T ／ F)

3. Japanese culinary culture is based on respect for nature and closely related to festivals and ceremonies.

   (T ／ F)

■ Multiple Choice

適切なものを（A）（B）（C）（D）より選びましょう。

1. In a statement, PM said he wants to _____ the Washoku culture to the future generation.
   (A) hand out   (B) hand away   (C) hand off   (D) hand down

2. The _____ will help soothe food safety concerns in the wake of the Fukushima nuclear accident triggered by the March 2011 earthquake and tsunami.
   (A) repercussion   (B) registration
   (C) resolution   (D) revolution

3. Japanese eating habits have become more and more _____.
   (A) sacrificed   (B) signified
   (C) diversified (D) modified

Practical Tips

- cuisineは、キッチンを意味するラテン語語源の単語で、「その地域や国の独特の料理法」といった意味で使われます。cooking, dietで代用することも可です。True or Falseの3問目には形容詞のculinaryも出題されています。
- 無形文化遺産の「無形」にはintangibleを使います。「触れることが出来ない」という語源で、「つかみどころがない、あいまいな」を意味するvagueの代用としても使えます。接頭語inを取ってtangibleになると、「有形の」「具体的な」です。English Compositionの3問目で実際に使ってみましょう。

Grammar Build-up

Incomplete Sentence

適切なものを（A）（B）（C）（D）より選び、文法上正しい英文を完成させましょう。

1. Managers' conference is held _____ a weekly basis.
   (A) for   (B) on   (C) in   (D) with

2. The intergovernmental panel is _____ representatives from several nations.
   (A) made up of   (B) lined up for
   (C) jumped out of   (D) kept up with

3. The sniper _____ the trigger without hesitation.
   (A) attacked   (B) placed   (C) took   (D) pulled

Rearrange in the Correct Order

順番を並べ替えて、意味の通る英文にしてください。（最初の文字は大文字に変更してください。）また、それを日本語にしましょう。

1. conference ／ Japan ／ an ／ played ／ in ／ the ／ important ／ role

   英文：＿＿＿＿＿＿＿＿＿＿＿＿＿＿＿＿＿＿＿＿＿＿
   訳：＿＿＿＿＿＿＿＿＿＿＿＿＿＿＿＿＿＿＿＿＿＿

2. diseases ／ deficiency ／ could ／ to ／ of ／ lead ／ the ／ vitamins

   英文：＿＿＿＿＿＿＿＿＿＿＿＿＿＿＿＿＿＿＿＿＿＿
   訳：＿＿＿＿＿＿＿＿＿＿＿＿＿＿＿＿＿＿＿＿＿＿

3. should ／ healthy ／ habits ／ people ／ eating ／ have

   英文：＿＿＿＿＿＿＿＿＿＿＿＿＿＿＿＿＿＿＿＿＿＿
   訳：＿＿＿＿＿＿＿＿＿＿＿＿＿＿＿＿＿＿＿＿＿＿

English-Japanese translation

次の英文の動詞を○で囲み、日本語にしましょう。

1. The intangible heritage system is aimed at protecting traditional performing arts, social practices and rituals.

2. The movement to add Article 9 of the Constitution as world heritage is underway.

3. Japanese officials are considering easing immigration rules to allow more foreigners to study Japanese cuisine.

Further Study

■ *Make sentences using the following words*

下の英単語の、ニュース本文の中で使われている品詞と意味を辞書で調べて書き、その単語が入った8ワード以上のオリジナルセンテンスを作りましょう。

	品詞	意味	その他の品詞や意味
1. respect	_____	_____	_____
2. appreciate	_____	_____	_____
3. boost	_____	_____	_____

■ *Speak up about the News*

以下の会話を聴き、空欄を埋めましょう。

Jijio: I'm (　　　　) now. I was not able to (　　　　) lunch and I (　　　　) my breakfast too.

Newcy: Really? We need three (　　　　) in a day; (　　　　), we would not be able to perform things well. I always have a Japanese style breakfast of a bowl of rice and miso soup in the morning. Japanese foods are not only (　　　　) but (　　　　) in calories. I'm so happy that Washoku has (　　　　) global recognition (　　　　).

Jijio: Yeah, that is good news. But since I am living (　　　　), preparing something to eat just for myself is (　　　　). I always (　　　　) (　　　　) the convenience stores for my meal.

■ *English Composition*

次の日本語を英語にしましょう。

1. 日本政府は、国内外で和食を宣伝してきた。　　　〔at home and abroad を使って〕

2. 日本人の生活様式と食習慣は、外国文化の影響もあって急激に変化してきた。〔lifestyles and dietary habits を使って〕

3. 私のコーチは目に見える結果にしか興味がない。〔tangible results を使って〕

28

第4章：セウォル号の悲劇

海外ニュース①

単語数：604
難度 ★★☆

Before Reading

救うことができたはずの前途ある多くの命が海上で断たれた。過積載。経験不足の船員による舵取り。待機を促す船内放送。真っ先に脱出した船長。船員の安全訓練に費やされた金額はわずか年間5万円。遺族の悔しさと悲しみは計り知れない。

■ Basic Vocabulary Building

英語に合う日本語を選びましょう。

1. unaccounted for ☐
2. freight ☐
3. comfirm ☐
4. desert ☐
5. submerge ☐

a. 見捨てる
b. 確認する
c. 浸水する
d. 貨物
e. 行方不明の

■ Advanced Vocabulary Building

英語に合う日本語を選びましょう。

1. treacherous ☐
2. distraught ☐
3. diminish ☐
4. wreckage ☐
5. theoretically ☐

a. 小さくなる
b. あてにならない
c. 残骸
d. 理論上は
e. 取り乱した

■ Pronunciation Training

アクセントのある母音に○をつけ、発音に注意して5回声に出して読んでみましょう。

1. desert（V）　2. witness　3. civilian　4. volunteer　5. vessel

Let's Read

Captain of Sunken South Korean Ferry Arrested by Police

Jindo, South Korea — South Korean police have formally arrested the captain and two crew members of a doomed ferry, on charges of deserting their passengers shortly after the vessel capsized Wednesday and sank.

Investigators allege the 69-year-old captain failed to carry out his duty to protect passengers when, according to witnesses, he was one of the first to leave the sinking ship. A report by South Korea's Yonhap news agency said the captain also is suspected of instructing passengers to remain seated, even as the ferry began rolling onto its side and blocking escape routes.

The ferry Sewol went down off the southwestern island of Jindo with 476 people on board.

Thirty-six people are confirmed dead, and 266 others — many of them high school students — remain unaccounted for as hope diminishes for finding more survivors. One hundred seventy-four others have been rescued, but none since Wednesday.

According to South Korean prosecutors, the 26-year-old third mate left to steer a doomed ferry through a treacherous waterway was navigating the area for the first time when the vessel listed on its side and sank with hundreds on board.

Yonhap reported that a team of 21 divers tried to enter a cabin on the submerged second deck of the five-deck ferry, where most of the passengers are believed to be trapped 35 meters below the surface. But the report said the divers, battling strong underwater currents, surfaced 14 minutes later without having gained entry.

More than 500 divers are working on the rescue teams. Many of them are civilian volunteers. Experts say people theoretically could survive for up to 72 hours if there are air pockets in the submerged compartments.

Authorities have not established the cause of the disaster. But some survivors report hearing a loud impact noise before the vessel rolled onto its side and began sinking.

The Yonhap report said the third officer is suspected of making a sharp turn while piloting the ship through a narrow route. Investigators are quoted as saying the sudden turn may have caused 180 vehicles and nearly 1,200 tons of freight to shift and disrupt the balance of the vessel before it began to list.

NOTES

doomed 破滅する運命にある
desert 見捨てる
capsize 転覆する
witness 目撃者

suspected of ～の疑いがある
roll onto one's side 横転する

confirm 確認する
unaccounted for 行方不明の
diminish 小さくなる

prosecutor 検察官
third mate 三等航海士
treacherous （天気などが）あてにならない
list 傾く

submerge 浸水する

civilian 市民
theoretically 理論上は

freight 貨物

Heavy fog was reported in the area on Tuesday evening, but it is not known whether that was a contributing factor.

President Barack Obama has sent his condolences to the families and says he will pay tribute to them during a visit to South Korea next week.

Meanwhile, hopes for survivors are fading. Anxiety and anger are growing among relatives of the missing, most of them high school students. Workers at Paengmok Harbor tried to console a parent of one of the missing high school children believed trapped inside the capsized ferry.

Despite earlier reports of success, rescue divers failed on their third day of attempting to get to passengers inside the ship, just 20 kilometers off shore. Oxygen was pumped into the ship in hopes it would reach any survivors. Divers later tried entering a cargo hold but were not able to go further, in a struggle against wreckage, strong currents and murky water.

Hundreds of volunteers and emergency workers at the harbor tried to comfort distraught relatives angry at the lack of progress and misinformation.

Parents of the missing demanded a road be cleared for any who might be rescued. Authorities quickly obliged, marching in a column of police.

Lee Min-seok, a rescue team captain with the Mokpo Firefighters, explained that the police presence is to keep crowds away so roads are clear enough for ambulances to pass through.

Several ambulances were readied nearby with flashing lights, but the display was cold comfort.

【April 19, 2014 | VOA】

NOTES

contributing factor 有力な要因
condolence 弔意
pay tribute 追悼する

console 慰める

oxygen 酸素

struggle もがき
wreckage （難破船の）残骸
murky 暗い
distraught 取り乱した
misinformation 誤報

ambulance 救急車

cold comfort 効き目のない慰め

BACKGROUND OF THE NEWS STORY

韓国仁川港から済州島へ向かっていた韓国最大の大型旅客船セウォル号（6825トン）が2014年4月16日、珍島沖で転覆し2時間半後に沈没した。船内から送られた携帯のメッセージには世界中が涙した。乗客乗員476人のうち、339人は修学旅行中の高校生325人と教員14人だった。293人が死亡、行方不明者11名（乗員は33人中23人救助）。乗客を避難誘導せず脱出した船長や、船員教育を怠った船会社代表らが逮捕、起訴された。

日本で18年間以上運航した後に韓国側に売却されたセウォル号は、客室が増築され、事故当時は規定の２倍の荷を積載していた。2013年２月に韓国史上初の女性大統領に就任した朴槿恵（パク・クネ）大統領（故朴正煕（パク・チョンヒ）元大統領の次女）の支持率は、沈没事故後一転した。大統領は涙の記者会見で、救難業務を怠った海洋警察を解体し、新たに国家安全庁を創設する方針を示した。

Comprehension Check

True or False

英文を日本語にし、ニュースの内容に合っていればT（True）、間違っていればF（False）に○をつけましょう。

1. All the passengers were rescued from the sunken vessel.

   _____ (T ／ F)

2. A 26-year-old third mate was left to steer the doomed ferry when the vessel listed on its side.

   _____ (T ／ F)

3. Most of the divers who are part of search and rescue, as well as with retrieval operation, are from the military.

   _____ (T ／ F)

Multiple Choice

適切なものを（A）（B）（C）（D）より選びましょう。

1. What is the first instruction that the passengers heard from the crews of the ship?
   - (A) Stay put.
   - (B) Please remain seated for the entire performance.
   - (C) Evacuate now.
   - (D) Don't panic and line up properly.

2. What is one of the main problems that the rescue divers are facing on their retrieval operation?
   - (A) salty water
   - (B) strong underwater currents
   - (C) a loud impact noise
   - (D) piranha

3. To which criminal act did the South Korean president compare the captain's decision of deserting the ferry and the passengers?
   - (A) libel
   - (B) homicide
   - (C) larceny
   - (D) murder

Practical Tips

- 海難ニュースによく出る単語には以下のようなものがあります。
  「傾く」= list, tilt, lean, careen。「転覆する」= capsize, keel。「沈没する」= submerge, sink。「難破船や難破船の残骸」= wreckage。「沈没船の引き上げ」= salvage です。
- 事故のニュースで、「死者数」は death tool、「死傷者数」は casuality です。「行方不明者」は missing のほか、本文でも使われている unaccounted for もよく見ます。直訳すると「説明がつかない」ですね。
- 「救急車」ambulance はフランス語で「歩く病院」という語源。「救急救命士」は paramedic です。

Grammar Build-up

Incomplete Sentence

適切なものを（A）（B）（C）（D）より選び、文法上正しい英文を完成させましょう。

1. Two hundred ninety-three people are confirmed dead and eleven others remain _____.
   (A) unaccounted for   (B) alive   (C) waiting for   (D) seated

2. The missing school children were believed trapped inside the _____ ferry.
   (A) capsize   (B) capsizes   (C) capsized   (D) capsizal

3. President Barack Obama has sent his _____ to the bereaved families.
   (A) personal letters   (B) congratulations
   (C) condolences   (D) credentials

Rearrange in the Correct Order

順番を並べ替えて、意味の通る英文にしてください。（最初の文字は大文字に変更してください。）また、それを日本語にしましょう。

1. rescued / vice / committed / the / later / suicide / principal
   英文：_____
   訳：_____

2. murder / a / they / facing / are / charge
   英文：_____
   訳：_____

3. rushing / I / ambulance / the scene / to / saw / an
   英文：_____
   訳：_____

English-Japanese translation

次の英文の動詞を○で囲み、日本語にしましょう。

1. The victims have shown signs of hypothermia after being exposed to very cold water temperature.

2. The ship was tilted at such an impossibly acute angle that the rescue workers couldn't reach the passengers' rooms.

3. Those who survived the accident flouted or did not follow the instructions given by the captain.

Further Study

Make sentences using the following words

下の英単語の、ニュース本文の中で使われている品詞と意味を辞書で調べて書き、その単語が入った8ワード以上のオリジナルセンテンスを作りましょう。

	品詞	意味	その他の品詞や意味
1. survivor	___	___	___
2. harbor	___	___	___
3. oblige	___	___	___

Speak up about the News

以下の会話を聴き、空欄を埋めましょう。

Jijio: Hi, Newcy. You seemed to be (　　　) reading something (　　　). What is it all about?

Newcy: Oh, I'm looking for any (　　　) regarding Sewol.

Jijio: Who is Sewol?

Newcy: No, silly. The Sewol is the ship that (　　　) near South Korea. The captain (　　　) his ship and passengers (　　　) (　　　). He was caught and now (　　　) murder charges.

Jijio: Oh, I see. That (　　　) me of what happened to "Titanic." The biggest (　　　) is that the captain stayed with the ship until the last moment.

Newcy: I feel sorry for the high schoolers and their families. They were just on their way to a happy (　　　) when it happened. They still had a lot of things (　　　) of them.

Voice your Opinion

In your opinion, in what situations do you think you should not follow rules given by authorities or those in higher position?

社会問題①

第5章：生殖医療の進歩と前途多難な法整備

単語数：588
難度 ★★★

Before Reading

　近年の生殖医療の急速な進歩で、性転換、代理母出産、凍結保存精子による死後懐胎などが可能になり、民法が制定された明治29年には想定できなかった親子関係が生じている。法整備が急がれるが、親子関係や倫理問題が絡み合い、日本の進む道はまだ見えない。

■ Basic Vocabulary Building

英語に合う日本語を選びましょう。

1. assumption　　　　a. 生殖医療
2. transgender　　　　b. 想定
3. reproductive medicine　　　　c. 害する
4. undermine　　　　d. 相続
5. inheritance　　　　e. 性の転換

■ Advanced Vocabulary Building

英語に合う日本語を選びましょう。

1. stipulate　　　　a. 補う、相殺する
2. deliberation　　　　b. 規定する
3. surrogacy　　　　c. 審議
4. compensate　　　　d. 授精
5. insemination　　　　e. 代理母であること

■ Pronunciation Training

アクセントのある母音に○をつけ、発音に注意して5回声に出して読んでみましょう。

1. erupt　　2. legitimate　　3. diversify　　4. differentiate　　5. spousal

Let's Read
Ruling LDP's debate on family expected to be rocky

The ruling Liberal Democratic Party's deliberations on family in light of developments in reproductive medicine and diversifying family values are expected to run into some bumps, as conservatives in the party continue to argue for the protection of the traditional family.

5   What touched off debate within the LDP was a Supreme Court ruling in December last year recognizing that a child born to a transgender man — who had suffered from a gender identity disorder and underwent a sex change operation — and his wife through sperm donation was their legitimate child under the Civil Code.

10   Protests erupted in the LDP's Judicial Affairs Division following the ruling, which challenged previously held assumptions on the definition of family. The division director, Taku Otsuka, emphasized the need to take quick action, saying, "The latest ruling will create wide-ranging confusion. We must quickly compensate for the 'holes' it has created."

15   In recent years, cases of children being born with third-party involvement such as artificial insemination using donated eggs or sperm or surrogacy for women who are unable to carry children has been on the rise around the world. However, existing Japanese laws have no clear stipulation on who the parents of a child born through such methods are.

20   To remedy this state of affairs, an LDP project team on assisted reproduction technologies is set to speed up deliberations toward new legislation and partial revision of the Civil Code in the next ordinary session of the Diet. The prospects of a resolution are unclear, however, since any attempt to recognize parent-child relationships between those 25 who are not biologically related is expected to draw objections from conservatives in the party.

    Toshiharu Furukawa, who heads the LDP project team, says, "There's a possibility we will allow LDP lawmakers to vote against party policy on related bills in the Diet."

30   Meanwhile, the issue of inheritance has become a renewed topic of debate. In September 2013, the Supreme Court ruled that a Civil Code article stipulating that a child born out of wedlock was entitled to receive only one-half the inheritance of a sibling born to married parents was unconstitutional. As a result, legislation to remove the discriminatory 35 clause from the Civil Code was passed in December 2013.

    The LDP leadership accepted the law revision, stating that not acting

---

NOTES

deliberation 審議
in light of ～を踏まえて
reproductive medicine 生殖医療
diversify 多様化する

touch off 引き起こす
Supreme Court 最高裁
transgender man 女性から男性への性転換者
gender identity disorder 性同一性障害 = GID
undergo (治療などを)受ける
sperm 精子
legitimate child 嫡出子
Civil Code 民法
erupt 勃発する
assumption 前提
compensate for ～を補う
artificial insemination 人工授精
surrogacy 代理母を務める事
stipulation 規定
remedy 直す
partial 部分的な
revision 訂正、修正
ordinary session of the Diet 通常国会
prospect 見通し
biologically 生物学的に

inheritance 相続

stipulate 規定する
child born out of wedlock 非嫡出子
entitle 資格を与える
sibling 兄弟姉妹
unconstitutional 違憲の

on the court decision would only result in more similar rulings. The party's conservatives have expressed dissatisfaction with the leadership's decision, however, contending that the move will undermine legal marriages and destroy the traditional family system. In response, a special committee on the protection of family ties was set up within the LDP, whose members called for a return to traditional family values at the committee's first meeting held on Dec. 19, 2013.

The special committee, in collaboration with a working team on inheritance laws that the Ministry of Justice is slated to set up this month, will spend the next year deliberating such measures as the protection of spousal residency rights at the time of inheritance and the division of an estate based on a spouse's "contributions." It remains unclear, however, whether legally differentiating spousal inheritance based on legal marriage aligns with the Japanese public's changing perspectives on family.

【January 09, 2014 │ Mainichi Japan】

NOTES

discriminatory clause 差別的な条項
contending 論争している
undermine 害する

in collaboration with ～と共同して
be slated to ～する予定である

spousal residency right 配偶者の居住権
estate 地所、財産
differentiate 差別化する
align with ～と協調する
perspective 視点

BACKGROUND OF THE NEWS STORY

　米フェイスブック（FB）は米国のユーザープロフィールに、従来のMale, Female以外のカスタマイズ性別を追加。「トランスジェンダー」や「インターセックス」など、合計なんと56パターン。FBは「自分自身のアイデンティティをうまく表現してもらいたい」と説明している。

　日本は戸籍法（1947年制定）に基づき、出生から死亡までの親子関係や婚姻関係を登録、公証している。ところが近年、生殖医療の進歩により、民法が想定しなかった親子関係が生じている。夫の死後、凍結保存した夫の精子で妻が妊娠し出産した裁判では、子は夫の法律上の子と認められなかった（2006年）。また芸能人夫婦が代理出産で得た子の裁判では、母子関係は分娩の事実により発生するという過去の判例を基に、母子関係の成立は認められなかった（2007年）。民法は「妻が婚姻中に懐胎した子は夫の子と推定する」と規定しているが、DNA鑑定により実際の血縁関係を明確することが可能になると複数の裁判が進行し、司法裁定の歯車がかみ合わないケースが多発している。子は社会の宝。生まれてくる子達が不利益を受けないためにも法の整備が急がれる。

Comprehension Check

True or False

英文を日本語にし、ニュースの内容に合っていればT（True）、間違っていればF（False）に〇をつけましょう。

1. The Japanese Civil Code is too old to cover modern-day issues of the family.

    (T ／ F)

2. The Supreme Court refused to recognize the boy as the transgender man's legitimate child as there's no biological link between them.

    (T ／ F)

3. The Supreme Court said that the discriminatory clause on the inheritance of an extra-marital child is legal.

    (T ／ F)

Multiple Choice

適切なものを（A）（B）（C）（D）より選びましょう。

1. Thanks to the advancement in _____, cases of children being born with third-party involvement have been on the rise.
    - (A) regenerative medicine
    - (B) herbal medicine
    - (C) reproductive medicine
    - (D) preventive medicine

2. What term refers to a strong and persistent feeling of discomfort with one's natural gender and self-identification towards the opposite sex?
    - (A) OCD
    - (B) PTSD
    - (C) ADHD
    - (D) GID

3. The sperm for artificial insemination may be obtained from the husband or from an anonymous _____.
    - (A) beneficiary
    - (B) donor
    - (C) sponsor
    - (D) recipient

Practical Tips

- 医学用語が多く難しいニュースですね。medicineは「薬」「医学」で、「生殖医療」はreproductive medicineです。in-vitro fertilization「体外受精」やartificial insemination「人工授精」などを行います。fertilizeは「受精させる」で、inseminateは「授精する」と、漢字が異なります。人工授精には、AIH = Artificial Insemination by Husband「配偶者［夫婦］間人工授精」と、AID = Artificial Insemination by Donor「非配偶者間人工授精」があります。
- undergoは「手術や治療などを受ける」です。undertake「仕事などを引き受ける」、undermine「（徐々に）衰えさせる、害する」と混同しないようにしましょう。
- 「通常国会」は本ニュースではordinary session of the Dietです。the Dietの代わりにParliamentもOKでその場合は無冠詞です。「臨時国会」はextraordinary sessionです。

Grammar Build-up

Incomplete Sentence

適切なものを（A）（B）（C）（D）より選び、文法上正しい英文を完成させましょう。

1. The summit meeting _____ to be held next month.
   (A) had slated　(B) slate　(C) slating　(D) is slated

2. The blockbuster Disney movie was produced in _____ with Pixar.
   (A) continuation　(B) collaboration　(C) compensation　(D) corrosion

3. The construction of an oil rig _____ a discord between the two countries.
   (A) touched off　(B) put off　(C) made off　(D) took off

Rearrange in the Correct Order

順番を並べ替えて、意味の通る英文にしてください。（最初の文字は大文字に変更してください。）また、それを日本語にしましょう。

1. up ／ mother ／ without ／ biological ／ he ／ grew ／ his

   英文：_____

   訳：_____

2. scandal ／ reputation ／ celebrity's ／ his ／ the ／ undermined

   英文：_____

   訳：_____

3. spousal ／ women ／ violence ／ many ／ are ／ suffering ／ from

   英文：_____

   訳：_____

English-Japanese translation

次の英文の動詞を○で囲み、日本語にしましょう。

1. A woman who was born through in-vitro fertilization in the 1970's had a natural pregnancy and delivery.

2. A group of patients filed a class action lawsuit with the district court against the hospital for compensation.

3. An Emmy award-winning actress had a surrogate mother give birth to her twin girls.

Further Study

Make sentences using the following words

下の英単語の、ニュース本文の中で使われている品詞と意味を辞書で調べて書き、その単語が入った8ワード以上のオリジナルセンテンスを作りましょう。

	品詞	意味	その他の品詞や意味
1. remedy	____	_____	_____
2. perspective	____	_____	_____
3. contend	____	_____	_____

Speak up about the News

以下の会話を聴き、空欄を埋めましょう。

Jijio: I saw a movie in which a father was (　　　　) to his family that he would become a woman.

Newcy: How is that (　　　　)? We can't change our gender, can we?

Jijio: We can. The advancement in transgender surgery and medicine (　　　　) people to do that.

Newcy: Oh, I see…but if my father would tell us about having a sex change, my mom would (　　　　).

Jijio: Nowadays, many people are suffering from gender (　　　　) issues called the GID. Such (　　　　) might help them live better lives.

Newcy: Even if it is (　　　　) possible, they might face a lot of (　　　　) like (　　　　) in the society.

Jijio: We should associate with them (　　　　) and (　　　　).

Voice your Opinion

It is said that Japanese couples opt for technology-assisted pregnancies instead of adoption. If so, what do you think are the reasons behind it?

教育・一般②

第6章：火山噴火でスヌーピー島出現!?

単語数：517
難度 ★★☆

Before Reading

　海底火山の噴火で、小笠原諸島に出現した新たな島。アメリカの人気コミックス『ピーナッツ』のキャラクター「スヌーピー」に形が似ているとネット上で話題となった。その後も噴火が続き、島の形は変わったが、このような微笑ましい"領土問題"は歓迎だ。

■ Basic Vocabulary Building

英語に合う日本語を選びましょう。

1. administer　　　　a. 塊状の、大きな
2. sovereignty　　　 b. 類似
3. cease　　　　　　c. 管理する
4. resemblance　　　d. 終わる
5. massive　　　　　e. 主権

■ Advanced Vocabulary Building

英語に合う日本語を選びましょう。

1. covet　　　　　　a. 合併する
2. volatility　　　　 b. 欲しがる
3. merge　　　　　　c. 腐食する
4. enchantment　　　d. 不安定さ
5. erode　　　　　　e. 歓喜、魅惑

■ Pronunciation Training

アクセントのある母音に○をつけ、発音に注意して5回声に出して読んでみましょう。

1. eruption　　2. sovereignty　　3. territorial　　4. aerial　　5. canine

Let's Read

Japanese 'Snoopy' island created by volcanic eruption

A volcanic eruption in Japan would usually have people living nearby reaching for their protective masks. But the recent formation of an island off the country's Pacific coast, after weeks of volcanic activity, has prompted more enchantment than fear at nature's volatility.

5　In the weeks since it rose from the sea 620 miles (1,000km) south of Tokyo, the island expanded amid continued volcanic activity, before merging with an existing island to create a new landmass with a remarkable resemblance to a cartoon dog — Snoopy.

The publication of aerial photos of Nishinoshima island and its new 10　addition prompted an outpouring of delight online.

The Kotaku blog noted that @tekken8810, one of many Twitter users who posted visual comparisons, called the island and its canine likeness a "complete match."

User @etienneeshrdlu joked: "Exactly as Nostradamus predicted. A 15　new Snoopy-shaped island rises from the sea near Tokyo," while @astralpouch declared: "Holy crap … Snoopy island … I don't care what they say I'm going over there."

Henceforth, the Japan-based Twitter-sphere deemed, the as-yet officially unnamed landmass would be known as Snoopy island.

20　Some speculated how long it would be before China claimed sovereignty over the island — a reference to a longstanding dispute over ownership of the Senkaku islands in the East China Sea.

Though meant as a joke, the comments did not entirely miss the mark: Japan plans to build port facilities and transplant fast-growing coral 25　fragments onto Okinotorishima, a pair of tropical islets located even farther south of Tokyo in a resource-rich area of ocean coveted by China.

And Japan's chief government spokesman, Yoshihide Suga, welcomed the prospect that Japan's borders could stretch, if only by a few hundred metres. "If it becomes an island, our country's territorial waters will 30　expand," he told reporters after the island was discovered last month.

By Christmas Eve, the island had expanded to about eight times its size when it was discovered, according to studies by Prof. Fukashi Maeno of Tokyo University's earthquake research institute.

A massive undersea volcanic eruption had resulted in the new island 35　linking with Nishinoshima at its two southern corners. In between sits a pool of reddish seawater — Snoopy's perfectly positioned collar.

NOTES

eruption 噴火
protective mask 防護マスク
volcanic activity 火山活動
prompt 刺激する
enchantment 歓喜、魅惑
volatility 変わりやすさ、不安定さ
merge 合体する
existing 既存の
landmass 陸塊
remarkable 注目すべき
resemblance 類似
aerial 空中の
outpouring （感情など の）ほとばしり
comparison 比較
canine 犬の
predict 予言する
holy crap （俗語）なんてこった

henceforth それ以降
sphere 領域
deem 〜と思う、みなす
speculate 推測する

sovereignty 主権
reference 言及
longstanding 積年の
miss the mark 的外れである
transplant 移植する
coral サンゴ
fragment かけら、一片
covet 欲しがる

prospect 展望、見通し
territorial waters 領海

massive 塊状の、大きな

Experts said that volcano remains highly active, as red magma continued to rise, raising the possibility that it will lose its endearing shape as it expands.

Uncertainty surrounds the long-term future of the new island, which for now forms part of the Ogasawara chain, also known as the Bonin islands, that are administered by Tokyo despite their distance from the Japanese capital.

Hiroshi Ito, a volcanologist with the Japanese coastguard, said the island could erode after the eruptions cease. "But it could also remain permanently," he told the FNN news network.

The last recorded volcanic eruption in the area occurred in 1974, according to the meteorological agency. Much of the volcanic activity happens under the sea, which is thousands of metres deep at the site of the Izu-Ogasawara-Marianas Trench.

No doubt aware of the media buzz surrounding Snoopy island, Japan's coastguard warned that the area was still very dangerous and told would-be tourists to stay away.

【Dec 30, 2013 │ By Justin McCurry — The Guardian】

NOTES

endearing かわいらしい

administer 管理する

volcanologist 火山学者
the Japanese coastguard 海上保安庁 正式名：Japan Coast Guard
erode 腐食する
cease 終わる
permanently 永遠に
meteorological agency 気象庁
trench 海溝
media buzz マスコミのうわさ
would-be 〜 自称〜の人、〜気取りの人
stay away 近づかない

BACKGROUND OF THE NEWS STORY

　東京から南に1000キロの太平洋沖合の海底火山が噴火し、噴出したマグマが冷え固まって新たな陸地を形成した。拡大を続けた陸地は既存の西之島と一体化。小笠原諸島に属する新たなこの島の形状が、アメリカの人気漫画『ピーナッツ』の主人公チャーリー・ブラウンの飼い犬スヌーピー（ビーグル犬）にそっくりだとネット上で話題になった。島の連結部分は赤みがかった海水だまりで、スヌーピーのカラーのようだとネチズン達は盛り上がった。

　領土問題と言えば、日本は韓国との間で竹島、中国とは尖閣諸島、ロシアとは北方領土をめぐる争いを解決できずにいる。アジアでは他に南沙諸島や西沙諸島でにらみ合い、インドとパキスタンは、カシミールの帰属先問題で過去に3度戦火を交えた。パレスチナ人難民問題も根底はイスラエル建国に端を発した領土問題だ。昨今はロシアとウクライナの間での緊張が続いている。領地と海洋の主権に関するニュースは、世界中どこでも、国家の醜い側面が浮き彫りになる交戦と悲劇の繰り返しだが、今回はなんとも微笑ましい「領土問題」である。

Comprehension Check

True or False

英文を日本語にし、ニュースの内容に合っていればT（True）、間違っていればF（False）に○をつけましょう。

1. The newly-discovered island connected with Okinotorishima Island.
   _____ (T／F)

2. The volcanic activities have ceased and experts predict that the island will remain its endearing shape.
   _____ (T／F)

3. The plan to make the new island tourist spots is underway.
   _____ (T／F)

Multiple Choice

適切なものを（A）（B）（C）（D）より選びましょう。

1. The _____ eruption created a new isle and it is getting bigger and bigger.
   (A) violence (B) volcanic (C) victorious (D) vicious

2. Japan plans to protect the island by building _____ facilities onto Okinotorishima island.
   (A) research (B) medical (C) military (D) port

3. There is a _____ dispute over ownership of the Senkaku island in the East China Sea.
   (A) civilian (B) human rights (C) territorial (D) legal

Practical Tips

- 「火山」はvolcanoで、「噴火する」はeruptです。「活火山」はactive volcano、「休火山」はdormant volcano、「死火山」はextinct volcanoです。
- 「似る」は、look like, be similar toの他、resembleも覚えておきたい単語です。他動詞なので、resemble toなどとしないように注意しましょう。
- would-beは名詞の前に置いて「〜になるつもりの、〜志望の、自称〜」です。English Composition 3問目の「見込み客」はwould-be customerとなります。少し堅くpotential customerやprospective customerとしてもいいですね。ちなみにwannabeになると「（アイドルのようになりたいと願う）熱狂的ファン」や「〜予備軍」です。
- 「犬」は通常はdogですが、イヌ科の動物を表すcanineをおどけて使う場合もあります。「ネコ（cat）」の場合はfeline。「鳥」はavian。「鳥インフルエンザ」はbird fluのほかavian fluとも言います。English-Japanese translation 2問目のk-9 dogはさて何のことでしょう？

Grammar Build-up

Incomplete Sentence

適切なものを (A) (B) (C) (D) より選び、文法上正しい英文を完成させましょう。

1. Experts predict it is _____ likely that the volcano in question remains active.
   (A) high   (B) highly   (C) higher   (D) height

2. The Organ _____ Law went into effect in October 1997.
   (A) Transport   (B) Transaction   (C) Transplant   (D) Transit

3. The party's new manifesto _____ and failed to attract people's attention.
   (A) missed the game   (B) missed the mark
   (C) missed the cut   (D) missed the bus

Rearrange in the Correct Order

順番を並べ替えて、意味の通る英文にしてください。(最初の文字は大文字に変更してください。) また、それを日本語にしましょう。

1. better ／ you'd ／ stay ／ from ／ away ／ troubles
   英文：_____
   訳：_____

2. and ／ buzzword-of-the-year ／ selected ／ is ／ annually ／ a ／ awarded
   英文：_____
   訳：_____

3. about ／ no ／ there ／ it ／ is ／ doubt
   英文：_____
   訳：_____

English-Japanese translation

次の英文の動詞を○で囲み、日本語にしましょう。

1. The 1953 ceasefire agreement between North and South Korea ended the Korean War.

2. K-9 dogs are trained to be good buddies of police officers.

3. Mt. Fuji is categorized as an active volcano.

Further Study

Make sentences using the following words

下の英単語の、ニュース本文の中で使われている品詞と意味を辞書で調べて書き、その単語が入った8ワード以上のオリジナルセンテンスを作りましょう。

	品詞	意味	その他の品詞や意味
1. prospect	_____	_____	_____
2. remarkable	_____	_____	_____
3. predict	_____	_____	_____

Speak up about the News

以下の会話を聴き、空欄を埋めましょう。

Newcy: Did you see the picture of the (　　　　) island? It's so cute and endearing.

Jijio: Yeah. I read Netizens' comments (　　　　). For Japan, it is good news because the island (　　　　) the territory of Japan.

Newcy: I (　　　　) with you. The island was formed due to volcanic (　　　　). Japan is a volcanic country, isn't it?

Jijio: Yes, there are many. One good thing about having volcanoes is we can enjoy (　　　　) (　　　　) (　　　　) all over the country. And they can be used for geothermal (　　　　)(　　　　). The downside is they may cause some (　　　　).

Newcy: Everything has (　　　　) and (　　　　).

English Composition

次の日本語を英語にしましょう。

1. アメリカの国土は日本の国土の約25倍だ。　　　　landmass を使って

2. 医者は患者に強い薬を投与した。　　　　administer を使って

3. いいセールスマンは常に見込み客の情報を管理している。　　　　would-be を使って

第 7 章：純国産人工知能ロケットイプシロン、未来に向けて発射！

テクノロジー②

単語数：491
難度 ★☆☆

Before Reading

　　日本の固体燃料ロケット技術の集大成、イプシロン。5番目のギリシャ文字に由来するその名には、Evolution & Excellence（革新・高性能）、Exploration（探査）などの想いも込められている。高性能と低コストを両立させ、次世代の宇宙輸送システムの鍵となる。

■ Basic Vocabulary Building

英語に合う日本語を選びましょう。

1. exploration　　　　　　a. 多数の
2. numerous　　　　　　　b. 望遠鏡
3. orbit　　　　　　　　　c. 探査
4. reliability　　　　　　　d. 軌道
5. telescope　　　　　　　e. 信頼性

■ Advanced Vocabulary Building

英語に合う日本語を選びましょう。

1. mainstay　　　　　　　a. 絶頂
2. predecessor　　　　　　b. 促進する
3. facilitate　　　　　　　c. 自律の
4. culmination　　　　　　d. 前任者
5. autonomous　　　　　　e. 主力の

■ Pronunciation Training

アクセントのある母音に○をつけ、発音に注意して5回声に出して読んでみましょう。

1. telescope　　2. ultraviolet　　3. rocket　　4. procedure　　5. atmosphere

Let's Read
Launch of the Epsilon rocket

The Japan Aerospace Exploration Agency on Sept. 14 launched the Epsilon, Japan's first new rocket in 12 years, putting the SPRINT-A planet-observation telescope into orbit some 1,000 km above the earth. The telescope uses extreme ultraviolet rays to observe the atmosphere of planets.

The successful rocket launch represents the culmination of Japan's solid-fuel rocket technology, which dates back to the tiny "pencil" rocket in the 1950s developed by the late Dr. Hideo Itokawa and his team. But JAXA and Japan's rocket industry have a long way to go to make the Epsilon rocket competitive enough in the international market of commercial satellite launches.

In developing the Epsilon rocket, the JAXA team aimed at smaller size, lower costs and higher capabilities.

The three-stage rocket, which is 24.4 meters high and 2.6 meters across and weighs 91 tons, is about half the height of JAXA's mainstay H-IIA rocket and is smaller than its predecessor M-5 rocket, which was retired in 2006 due to its high cost.

To lower the production cost, no new engines were designed. Instead, the Epsilon utilizes the H-IIA's solid-fuel booster and parts of the M-5. But it makes full use of advanced IT technology.

About 100 people used to work in a large room to control the launch of a rocket. But in the launch of the Epsilon, only three were required to inspect the rocket with two personal computers. Artificial intelligence carried out autonomous pre-launch checks of the vehicle composed of numerous parts. This is an application of technology used in the machinery industry. The "mobile control" of a rocket launch was the first attempt in the world. The traditional control room near a launch pad became unnecessary.

In the past, it took JAXA 42 days from the time of setting up a rocket in a launch pad to the removal of related equipment after a launch. In the launch of the Epsilon, the period was shortened to seven days. Simplifying the procedure needed for a rocket launch is an important factor for facilitating a successful launch.

To reduce the weight of the Epsilon, light materials including carbon fiber were used in parts. JAXA successfully launched the rocket after three years of development. Thus Japan's solid-fuel rocket technology

NOTES

Japan Aerospace Exploration Agency 宇宙航空研究開発機構 ＝ JAXA
telescope 望遠鏡
orbit 軌道
ultraviolet rays 紫外線
atmosphere 大気（圏）
culmination 頂点、絶頂
solid-fuel 固体燃料の
competitive 競争力がある

three-stage 3段の
mainstay 主力の
predecessor 前任者

utilize 利用する

autonomous 自律の
compose 構成する
numerous 多数の

launch pad 発射台

facilitate 促進する
material 素材
carbon fiber 炭素繊維

was revived seven years after the M-5 rocket was retired. Seven M-5 rockets were launched from 1997 to 2006.

From now on, solid-fuel rockets will be launched from the Uchinoura Space Center and liquid-fuel rockets from the Tanegashima Space Center, both in Kagoshima Prefecture.

At ¥5.3 billion, the cost of the first Epsilon was about 70 percent of the cost of the M-5 rocket. JAXA hopes to reduce the cost to ¥3 billion by 2017. But it is not easy to compete in the international market. At the very least, JAXA will need to prove the reliability of the Epsilon rocket by increasing the number of launches. JAXA and Japan's rocket industry must further improve the technology for easy-to-launch rockets.

【Sep 23, 2013 | The Japan Times】

NOTES

liquid-fuel 液体燃料の

reliability 信頼性

BACKGROUND OF THE NEWS STORY

　2013年9月14日、午後2時、鹿児島県内之浦宇宙空間観測所の発射筒から、新型固体燃料ロケット「イプシロン」1号機が発射された。1時間後、搭載された惑星分光観測衛星「SPRINT-A」の宇宙軌道への進入が確認され、打ち上げは成功した。この観測衛星は内之浦で最初に朝日があたる岬の名にちなみ「ひさき」と命名された。JAXAとIHIエアロスペースが205億円をかけて共同開発したイプシロンは全長24.4m、直径2.6m、重さ91tの3段固体燃料ロケットで1.2tの小型衛星を軌道に投入できる。
　日本の独自開発新型ロケットの発射は、2001年8月液体燃料ロケットH-2Aの打ち上げ以来であった。世界最高レベルの性能を誇ったM5の後継機として開発されたイプシロンは、点検と管制業務のコンピューター管理により、M5では100人体制で42日間要した発射準備作業を、2人が7日間で終えることを可能にした。総発射費用はM5の半分の30億円とコストパフォーマンスがよく、軽量のイプシロンは、官民一体で宇宙ビジネスの国際競争力を高める日本の努力のシンボルであり、量産に適した次世代ロケットとして世界的に注目されている。

Comprehension Check

▣ *True or False*

英文を日本語にし、ニュースの内容に合っていればT（True）、間違っていればF（False）に○をつけましょう。

1. The Epsilon is the first rocket the Japan Aerospace Exploration Agency has made.

   _____ （T ／ F）

2. This rocket is the new stage of rocket technology after the expensive solid-fuel ones were retired in 2006.

   _____ （T ／ F）

3. The "mobile control" technology makes it possible for only three people to inspect the Epsilon launch.

   _____ （T ／ F）

▣ *Multiple Choice*

適切なものを（A）（B）（C）（D）より選びましょう。

1. The _____ of a rocket launch was the first attempt in the world.
   - (A) manual control
   - (B) birth control
   - (C) gun control
   - (D) mobile control

2. What is the light material used on most parts of the rocket?
   - (A) platinum
   - (B) carbon fiber
   - (C) alloy
   - (D) optic fiber

3. The main mission for Epsilon is to _____ .
   - (A) put a telescope into orbit
   - (B) lift off a ballistic missile
   - (C) boost a space shuttle into orbit
   - (D) launch a manned spacecraft

Practical Tips

- ロケット関連ニュースで必ず使われる単語はlaunch「打ち上げる」です。ロケット以外にも「船を進水させる、新事業を開始する、新製品を売り出す」など、勢いよく何かをスタートさせる場合に使います。母音の読み方に注意をしましょう。
- launchの他に、ロケット打ち上げに使われる語は、lift offやblast offなどです。
- telescope「望遠鏡」は、tele「遠距離、電信」＋scope「見ること」から成る語。microscopeだと「顕微鏡」、endoscopeだと「内視鏡」。
- retireは「（通例定年で）退職、引退する」場合に使います。「船や飛行機の就役を解く」decommissionという語もあります。バイトなど短期間働いてやめる時はquitです。

Grammar Build-up

Incomplete Sentence

適切なものを（A）（B）（C）（D）より選び、文法上正しい英文を完成させましょう。

1. The asteroid 25143 Itokawa was named _____ Dr. Hideo Itokawa.
   (A) after   (B) for   (C) as   (D) with

2. You should _____ the most of your opportunities.
   (A) have   (B) give   (C) make   (D) take

3. The Galapagos phones are _____ of smartphones.
   (A) founders   (B) predecessors   (C) mentors   (D) successors

Rearrange in the Correct Order

順番を並べ替えて、意味の通る英文にしてください。（最初の文字は大文字に変更してください。）また、それを日本語にしましょう。

1. summer / Häagen-Dazs / campaign / a / launched

   英文：_____

   訳：_____

2. NASA / Japanese / counterpart / JAXA / is / of / the

   英文：_____

   訳：_____

3. the Big Mac / a / of / mainstay / is / product / McDonalds

   英文：_____

   訳：_____

English-Japanese translation

次の英文の動詞を○で囲み、日本語にしましょう。

1. The rocket carrying a planet-observation satellite blasted off from the Uchinoura Space Center in Kagoshima Prefecture.

2. The satellite equipped with a space telescope will remotely observe planets such as Venus, Mars and Jupiter.

3. Working as a TV commentator can be a launching pad for going into politics.

Further Study

■ Make sentences using the following words

下の英単語の、ニュース本文の中で使われている品詞と意味を辞書で調べて書き、その単語が入った8ワード以上のオリジナルセンテンスを作りましょう。

		品詞	意味	その他の品詞や意味
1.	retire	————	————	————————————
2.	atmosphere	————	————	————————————
3.	utilize	————	————	————————————

■ Speak up about the News

以下の会話を聴き、空欄を埋めましょう。

Newcy: Hey, Jijio. do you know Kirobo?

Jijio: Yes, It's the first talking robot to (   ) astronauts (   ).

Newcy: It's so (   )! I hope I can have one.

Jijio: I hope I can have a rocket that can take me to (   ), maybe something like the Epsilon rocket.

Newcy: What is that? Is it a kind of ballistic (   )? That would be (   )!

Jijio: Are you serious? Of course not. It's a solid-fuel rocket that (   ) developed. It's smaller in size, fully (   ) and has higher capabilities compared to its (   ).

Newcy: I don't know much about space science, but I can say the (   ) in technology is (   ). It definitely is one thing that Japan can be (   ) (   ).

■ Voice your Opinion

Why do some countries spend huge amounts of money into space technology? How do you see the significance of space technology?

文化・芸能②

第8章：宝塚歌劇団100周年

単語数：516
難度 ★★☆

Before Reading

　「清く・正しく・美しく」をモットーに、1世紀にわたり夢の舞台を作り上げてきた宝塚歌劇団。未来のタカラジェンヌを夢見る少女達は、今年も狭き門（2014年志願倍率：26.6倍（「神戸新聞」2014年3月29日より））の宝塚音楽学校に挑む。

Basic Vocabulary Building

英語に合う日本語を選びましょう。

1. plot　　　　　　　a. 持ちこたえる
2. found　　　　　　b. 年長
3. endure　　　　　　c. 設立する
4. evoke　　　　　　d. 筋
5. seniority　　　　　e. 喚起する

Advanced Vocabulary Building

英語に合う日本語を選びましょう。

1. flamboyant　　　　a. 異性の服装を着ること
2. gigantic　　　　　b. 華やかな
3. aristocrat　　　　　c. 厳しく統制された
4. regimented　　　　d. 巨人のような
5. cross-dressing　　　e. 貴族

Pronunciation Training

アクセントのある母音に○をつけ、発音に注意して5回声に出して読んでみましょう。

1. centennial　　2. thrilling　　3. vaudeville　　4. premiere　　5. romance

53

Let's Read

A century on stage

Osaka — The all-woman Takarazuka Revue marked 100 years of leg-kicking, cross-dressing, singing, dancing and thrilling audiences on April 1.

A special performance by the all-woman company is now playing a run at the Takarazuka Grand Theater in Takarazuka, Hyogo Prefecture.

During the show, which started March 21, 100 dancers in costumes evoking pink roses form a flamboyant chorus line in front of a gigantic birthday cake. It's vaudeville meets Moulin Rouge, with a little Japaneseness in the mix.

Among the dancers are 39 women from the 100th class of the Takarazuka Music School, who graduated March 1.

Revolutionary revue

The three-part Moon Troupe 100th anniversary program runs until April 28 at the Takarazuka Grand Theater and from May 16 to June 15 at the Tokyo Takarazuka Theater.

Takarazuka was founded in 1913 by Ichizo Kobayashi, the founder of Hankyu, a major railway operator based in Osaka. He brought the women together hoping to attract people to his hot-spring resorts. The company was the first in Japan to present a revue, a show combining music, dance and drama. It grew steadily, opening a theater in Tokyo and performing overseas.

"The Rose of Versailles," a tragic love story set during the French Revolution, is one of its most popular performances. The musical was a sensation when it premiered in 1974, and is now regarded as a "Takarasienne" classic.

Playwright and director Shinji Ueda's long efforts to keep the play fresh have helped it endure. When new actresses take on major parts, he revises the plot to play to their strengths.

The play tells the story of a romance between Oscar, a female aristocrat raised as a man, and Andre, her less wealthy foster brother. It also explores an ill-fated relationship between Marie Antoinette, the queen of France, and Swedish Count Hans Axel von Fersen.

The musical was adapted from Riyoko Ikeda's manga comic book of the same name. Ueda rewrote it for the stage because of the popularity of the manga among women. Versions of the play that focus on von Fersten and also on Oscar and Andre have been performed.

Popular tradition

Performance style is passed from generation to generation for the most famous scenes. "The Rose of Versailles" has brought 4.77 million people to theaters in total.

Takarazuka consists of five troupes, which take turns performing the plays. In commemoration of the 100th anniversary of its foundation, the company is spending extra time and money on special effects for the performance.

Takarazuka's success is based on its regimented and seniority-based system of training and recruitment. "Senior students teach juniors about how to behave," said Kazuo Sumi, chairman of Hankyu. "This helps pass down the Takarazuka traditions and deepen ties among classmates. More than 1,300 graduates attended a ceremony last year for the school's centennial. Takarazuka is as much a family as a company."

Takarazuka's first independent staging abroad took place last year in Taiwan. The run made a slight profit from box office revenues and income from sponsors, Sumi said.

"We will strive to preserve Takarazuka and to evolve," he said. "It is beloved by many people."

【April 10, 2014 | Nikkei】

NOTES

consist of ～から構成される
troupe 一座、一団
take turns 交代で行う
commemoration 記念
special effects 特撮効果
regimented 厳しく統制された
seniority-based 年功序列の
centennial 100年祭、100周年
box office revenue 興行収入
strive 努力する
beloved 愛される

BACKGROUND OF THE NEWS STORY

　宝塚ファミリーランド（2003年8月31日営業終了）の前身、「宝塚新温泉」が開業したのが1911年。その2年後に、阪急創業者の小林一三氏の提案により、不人気で閉鎖となった室内プールを改装した劇場が作られ、アトラクションのための少女歌劇「宝塚唱歌隊」が結成された。その後「宝塚音楽歌劇学校」「宝塚音楽舞踊学校」と改名され、現在は「宝塚音楽学校」となっている。
　高倍率の難関を乗り越えた音楽学校の生徒達は予科と本科の2年の間に、音楽や舞踊や演劇を徹底的に学び、校訓「清く、正しく、美しく」の教えに基づき、礼儀作法やマナーを磨かれる。平成25年（2013年）に創立100周年を迎えた宝塚歌劇団は、宝塚音楽学校の卒業生の未婚女性だけで構成される。この1世紀の間に音楽学校の卒業生、約4500名が舞台を踏んできた。1914年の初公演以来、年間公演数約1300回、観客動員数約250万人、歌劇団員総数約400人。現在は花・月・雪・星・宙の5組と、いずれの組にも所属しない専科に分かれている。男性の役を「男役」、女性の役を「娘役」と呼ぶ。演目は古今東西、歴史物からファンタジーと多岐に渡る。

Comprehension Check

◻ *True or False*

英文を日本語にし、ニュースの内容に合っていればT（True）、間違っていればF（False）に○をつけましょう。

1. Shows of the Takarazuka Revue are performed exclusively by females.
   _____
   （T ／ F）

2. "The Rose of Versailles" is one of the signature programs of the Takarazuka Revue.
   _____
   （T ／ F）

3. The Takarazuka Revue was founded by the owner of a leading steel enterprise.
   _____
   （T ／ F）

◼ *Multiple Choice*

適切なものを（A）（B）（C）（D）より選びましょう。

1. What is the meaning of "Revue"?
   - (A) a show combining music, dance and drama
   - (B) a process of re-checking and re-evaluation
   - (C) a group of cross-dressers
   - (D) a magic and illusion show

2. Founded in 1913, the company celebrated its _____ in 2014.
   - (A) golden anniversary　(B) jubilee　(C) millennium　(D) centennial

3. The aim of establishing the Takarazuka Revue was to _____.
   - (A) honor the achievements of the late city major
   - (B) preserve the cultural heritage of the place
   - (C) draw visitors to the Takarazuka city
   - (D) create job opportunities for the residents

Practical Tips

- 宝塚歌劇団の正式英語名はTakarazuka Revue。Revueはフランス語で、歌や踊りや劇で構成されるミュージカル・バラエティー・ショーです。（Multiple Choice 1問目の大ヒント！）同じ発音のreviewと混同しないようにしましょう。
  また、歌劇団の言い換えで本文中に使われているcompanyとtroupeは、共に「（バレエや劇団やサーカスの）一座」に使われる語です。troupeはtroop（軍隊）と同じ発音です。
- 『ベルサイユのばら』に描かれるマリー・アントワネットとフェルゼンのill-fated「不運な、不幸な」ロマンス。fateは人知を超えた絶対不可避な運命の力で、destinyやdoomよりも口語的です。薄幸の恋人たちを表すには、star-crossed loversという表現もあります。
- 「（そのままの状態で）採用、導入する」はadoptで、これに似たadaptは「適応させる」です。the musical adapted from Riyoko Ikeda's manga comic book of the same name.（p.54, ℓ.32）は、「池田理代子原作の同名の漫画を元に脚色したミュージカル」となります。

Grammar Build-up

Incomplete Sentence

適切なものを（A）(B)(C)(D) より選び、文法上正しい英文を完成させましょう。

1. _____ graduating from the school, the gender role of each member is finalized.
   (A) As (B) Upon (C) With (D) When

2. We can see many enthusiastic fans _____ for a glimpse of their heartthrob stars.
   (A) waiting (B) wait (C) to wait (D) waited

3. The ceremony closed _____ alumnae singing their school anthem together.
   (A) for (B) with (C) when (D) but

Rearrange in the Correct Order

順番を並べ替えて、意味の通る英文にしてください。（最初の文字は大文字に変更してください。）また、それを日本語にしましょう。

1. made ／ five ／ is ／ up ／ the Revue ／ troupes ／ of

   英文：_____

   訳：_____

2. important ／ training ／ is ／ cross-cultural

   英文：_____

   訳：_____

3. is ／ the seniority ／ a ／ the past ／ system ／ of ／ thing

   英文：_____

   訳：_____

English-Japanese translation

次の英文の動詞を○で囲み、日本語にしましょう。

1. After passing the highly competitive entrance examination of Takarazuka Musical School, students must take rigorous lessons before joining the Takarazuka Revue.

2. Dressed in traditional black kimono bearing a family crest and "hakama" pleated skirts, each student received a diploma from the school's principal.

3. The philosophy of the Takarazuka Theater Troupe is "Purity, Honesty and Beauty."

Further Study

Make sentences using the following words

下の英単語の、ニュース本文の中で使われている品詞と意味を辞書で調べて書き、その単語が入った8ワード以上のオリジナルセンテンスを作りましょう。

	品詞	意味	その他の品詞や意味
1. run	___	___	___
2. company	___	___	___
3. raise	___	___	___

Speak up about the News

以下の会話を聴き、空欄を埋めましょう。

Newcy: I went to see a (   ) by the Takarazuka theater group last week. I was really (   ).

Jijio: Really? I heard that they have an (   ) cast. Don't you think that's (   )?

Newcy: (   )(   )(   ). They were all very (   ).

Jijio: Also, I heard that the training is very hard as well.

Newcy: That's true. Not only the training itself (   ) (   ) the discipline. The training (   ) on developing their skills (   ) the discipline polishes their character. Trainees start their day by (   ) the practice hall.

English Composition

次の日本語を英語にしましょう。

1. 宝塚歌劇団は1938年の初の海外公演以来、17か国で24回公演を行った。

   　ノーヒント！

2. 悲劇の恋物語『ベルサイユのバラ』は、フランス革命時の貴族の生活に触れている。

   　aristocrats と French Revolution を使って

3. 退団後、すべてのタカラジェンヌ達は、第二の人生を選ぶという岐路に立つ。

   　stand at the crossroad を使って

第9章：謎に包まれたJFK暗殺から半世紀

海外ニュース②

単語数：491
難度 ★★☆

Before Reading

　1963年11月22日。テキサス州ダラスの快晴の空に銃弾が響き、第35代米国大統領、ジョン・F・ケネディの命が絶たれた。若く人望ある大統領の突然の死は、半世紀が経過した今もなお、国民的悲劇として人々の心に刻まれ、陰謀説が暗い影を落としている。

Basic Vocabulary Building

英語に合う日本語を選びましょう。

1. mission
2. collide
3. ambitious
4. interaction
5. diverse

a. 衝突する
b. 野心的な
c. 使命、任務
d. 多様な
e. 交流、相互作用

Advanced Vocabulary Building

英語に合う日本語を選びましょう。

1. segregate
2. poignant
3. commemoration
4. podium
5. blustery

a. 風が激しく吹く
b. 分離する
c. 痛切な
d. 祝典
e. 演壇

Pronunciation Training

アクセントのある母音に○をつけ、発音に注意して5回声に出して読んでみましょう。

1. assassin　2. tragedy　3. bullet　4. participant　5. frontier

Let's Read

Dallas Observes 50th Anniversary of Kennedy Assassination

Dallas — On a cold, rainy day, thousands of people gathered in Dallas, Texas, to honor the memory of President John F. Kennedy near the spot where he was killed 50 years ago by a sniper. Friday's commemoration focused not on the tragedy, but on the inspiration Kennedy provided to people around the world.

The simple ceremony took place in Dealey Plaza next to Elm Street, where an assassin's bullets ended the life of President Kennedy. That tragic day was bright and sunny, but the commemoration took place under cloudy skies, with participants bracing against cold, blustery winds and light rain.

For Dallas, this was an especially poignant moment, as the city has struggled for decades to remove the stigma of the assassination. Dallas Mayor Mike Rawlings said that "hope and reality" collided on that day in his city, but that the city has grown and changed, partly because of the inspirations Kennedy provided.

"Today, because of the hard work of many people, Dallas is a different city. I believe the new frontier did not die that day on our Texas frontier," said Rawlings.

Kennedy's inspiring and youthful image also was recalled when historian David McCullough took the podium. "He was young to be president, but it did not seem so if you were younger still. He was ambitious to make it a better world and so were we."

That Kennedy spirit is what drew people, young and old, to brave the weather and attend the ceremony in Dealey Plaza. Miguel Andrews was a five-year-old living with his parents in Mexico City when President Kennedy was assassinated. He credits Kennedy for setting ambitious goals, like the mission to the moon.

"He really drove the will of the Americans to go to the moon. I don't think anyone could have done or inspired this to be done in less than 10 years," he said.

U.S. astronauts landed on the moon nearly six years after JFK's death and many of his other projects, like civil rights, also took effect in the years following his assassination in Dallas.

Dallas resident Charlene Wyatt was 12 years old 50 years ago, but she credits Kennedy for having proposed the civil rights legislation that would later allow black people like her to fully participate in society.

NOTES

commemoration 祝典
inspiration 刺激

assassin 暗殺者
bullet 弾丸

participant 参加者
brace 備える
blustery 風が激しく吹く = blusterous
poignant 痛切な
struggle 苦心する
stigma 汚名
assassination 暗殺
collide ぶつかる

frontier 辺境

take the podium 登壇する

ambitious 野心的な
brave 勇敢に立ち向かう

credit ～の功績を認める

mission 使命、任務

civil rights 公民権
take effect 効力を発する

"We got a greater sense of being able to do things that we were not able to do before, go to school, get degrees and stuff."

In 1963, Dallas and most of the southern U.S. states were racially segregated, but Dallas today is a diverse city where interaction among races and nationalities is common. The city is twice the size it was then, with a metropolitan area population, including the nearby city of Fort Worth, of more than 6 million people. Dealey Plaza, the museum in the building where the assassin fired, and the nearby John F. Kennedy Memorial, will remain to remind people of the crime and the man whose promise was cut short.

【Nov 22, 2013 │ VOA】

NOTES

degree 学位

segregate 分離する
diverse 多様な
interaction 交流、相互作用

BACKGROUND OF THE NEWS STORY

　ジョン・F・ケネディは1917年に生まれた、カトリック信者、アイルランド系としての初の米大統領であった。在任中には、ピッグス湾事件、キューバ危機、ベルリンの壁の建設、米ソの宇宙開発競争、公民権運動の高まり、ベトナム戦争早期撤退計画の発表など多くの歴史的事件が発生した。

　1963年11月22日にテキサス州ダラスで起きた暗殺事件を、政府の調査委員会は、元海兵隊員、リー・オズワルドの単独犯行と断定したが、暗殺シーンの8ミリ映像や、緊急治療を行った医師の証言が委員会の報告とは合致しない不可解な点が残り、なによりも暗殺2日後にオズワルドが射殺されたことを口封じと見る向きもあり、多くの米国民は、CIA、マフィア、軍事産業界、当時のソ連などの「真犯人」の存在を信じている。JFKの実弟ロバートは、兄の暗殺後、NY州の上院議員にも選出されたが、1968年に大統領候補指名選の最中に42歳で暗殺。JFKジュニアは、38歳の時に妻と共に飛行機事故で死亡。

　未亡人となったジャックリーンは、悲劇の5年後、ギリシャの大富豪オナシスと再婚。1994年癌で死去。長女のキャロラインは現駐日米大使である。

Comprehension Check

◻ *True or False*

英文を日本語にし、ニュースの内容に合っていればT（True）、間違っていればF（False）に○をつけましょう。

1. Dallas marked the 60th death anniversary of JFK last November 22, 2013.
   _____
   （T ／ F）

2. Dealey Plaza in Dallas, Texas, where the shooter allegedly fired at JFK, is now demolished.
   _____
   （T ／ F）

3. JFK proposed the civil rights legislation that would later allow black people to fully participate in society.
   _____
   （T ／ F）

◻ *Multiple Choice*

適切なものを（A）（B）（C）（D）より選びましょう。

1. The _____ is the location of JFK's assassination.
   - (A) Fair Park Texas
   - (B) Dealey Plaza
   - (C) San Antonio Missions National Historical Park
   - (D) Bastrop State Park

2. What is one of the most ambitious goals that JFK set during his term?
   - (A) mission to Mars
   - (B) mission to Venus
   - (C) ISS Program
   - (D) mission to the moon

3. Jacqueline Kennedy was 31 when she entered the _____ and became a widow at 34.
   - (A) White House
   - (B) Kremlin
   - (C) Blue House
   - (D) Downing Street

Practical Tips

- assassin「暗殺者」は、大麻の力を借りて暗殺を企てたことより、アラビア語の大麻常用者が語源。assassinatorもOKだが、assassinの方が使用頻度は高いです。assassinationは「暗殺」で、動詞はassassinate「暗殺する」。
- 「射殺される」を英語にすると、be shot to deathかbe shot deadあるいは、be gunned downでもOKです。
- English-Japanese translation 3問目のニール・アームストロングの月面着陸後の有名な言葉と、Speak up about the NewsのNewcyが引用するケネディのスピーチ引用の後に［sic］と書かれています。これは「原文のまま」という意味の副詞です。誤りや疑いのある原文をそのまま引用する場合、引用語句の後に［sic］と記します。

Grammar Build-up

Incomplete Sentence

適切なものを (A) (B) (C) (D) より選び、文法上正しい英文を完成させましょう。

1. The commemorative ceremony _____ under overcast sky.
   (A) took care of   (B) took place   (C) took the podium   (D) took off

2. You should _____ risks by asking for a second opinion.
   (A) diversify   (B) unify   (C) modify   (D) clarify

3. My family loves eating pasta, which reminds us _____ our home country.
   (A) to   (B) in   (C) with   (D) of

Rearrange in the Correct Order

順番を並べ替えて、意味の通る英文にしてください。（最初の文字は大文字に変更してください。）また、それを日本語にしましょう。

1. gay ／ to be ／ I ／ think ／ a stigma ／ don't ／ it is

   英文：_____

   訳：_____

2. popular ／ is ／ alike ／ old ／ among ／ young ／ Facebook ／ and

   英文：_____

   訳：_____

3. dominated ／ Japanese ／ athletes ／ podium ／ the

   英文：_____

   訳：_____

English-Japanese translation

次の英文の動詞を○で囲み、日本語にしましょう。

1. Caroline Kennedy, the U.S. ambassador to Japan, was five days shy of her sixth birthday when her father was killed on Nov. 22, 1963.

2. Nelson Mandela was highly respected around the world for his long struggle to end the racist segregation in South Africa.

3. The astronaut was quoted as saying "That's one small step for [a] man, one giant leap for mankind." [sic]

Further Study

■ *Make sentences using the following words*

下の英単語の、ニュース本文の中で使われている品詞と意味を辞書で調べて書き、その単語が入った8ワード以上のオリジナルセンテンスを作りましょう。

	品詞	意味	その他の品詞や意味
1. degree	____	_____	_____
2. common	____	_____	_____
3. interaction	____	_____	_____

■ *Speak up about the News*

以下の会話を聴き、空欄を埋めましょう。

Jijio: Who is your (　　　　) US president?

Newcy: I like JFK, or President John F. Kennedy the most. I was (　　　　) by the phrase he used in his speech, which was "Ask not (　　　　) your country can do for you, [but] ask (　　　　) you can do for your country. [sic]"

Jijio: It was a big (　　　　) for the United States for such a president to be gone (　　　　) (　　　　). He (　　　　) (　　　　) at the age of 46.

Newcy: Many Americans see the Kennedys as a kind of American (　　　　) (　　　　). Kennedy family members have been (　　　　) a lot of attention.

Jijio: Their family has had many (　　　　) called the "Kennedy Curse."

■ *English Composition*

次の日本語を英語にしましょう。

1. 島民たちは、接近している台風に備えていた。　　　　[brace を使って]

2. 1980年、ジョン・レノンは、ファンの一人によって射殺された。

    [Practical Tips2 番を参考に]

3. 多方面からの反対にもかかわらず、「秘密保護法」が成立した。　　[take effect を使って]

社会問題②

第10章：スマホの危険から子供を守るには？

単語数：524
難度 ★★☆

Before Reading

　学年が上がるにつれて使用者の割合も増え、子供の欲しいものランキング上位に常に食い込む「スマートフォン」。親との連絡手段、友達とのコミュニケーションなどの利便性は否定できないが、非行や犯罪に巻き込まれるきっかけとなる危険とも隣り合わせだ。

■ Basic Vocabulary Building

英語に合う日本語を選びましょう。

1. giant □　　　　　　a. 装置
2. identity theft □　　b. 明らかにする
3. device □　　　　　c. 誤解
4. reveal □　　　　　d. 大企業
5. misconception □　　e. 個人情報の盗難

■ Advanced Vocabulary Building

英語に合う日本語を選びましょう。

1. bully □　　　　　　a. 委託する
2. immune □　　　　　b. 傷つきやすい
3. unwittingly □　　　c. いじめる
4. commission □　　　d. 知らず知らずに
5. vulnerable □　　　e. 免疫のある

■ Pronunciation Training

アクセントのある母音に○をつけ、発音に注意して5回声に出して読んでみましょう。

1. appropriate　2. vulnerable　3. survey　4. purchase　5. parental

65

Let's Read

Parents unaware of dangers faced by children on smartphones

Many parents are out of touch with the dangers faced by their children on tablets and smartphones, according to a poll by BBC Learning.

Almost one in five children said they had seen something on their devices that had upset them, twice the number parents had thought.

5　A separate study found that just over 20% of parents do not monitor what their children are doing online.

The research was commissioned as part of Safer Internet Day.

While 90% of the parents surveyed by the BBC in England said they had spoken to their children about staying safe online when using a tablet
10　or a smartphone, most said they allowed their children to use them unsupervised.

Parental controls

"Unfortunately, none of us — of whatever age — is immune from encountering problems online," said Tony Neate, chief executive of Get Safe Online.

15　"Without using controls such as built-in security, safety and privacy features and search engine filters, children will almost certainly run into something that really isn't appropriate for their age, or any age."

The survey also found that teenagers aged 13-16 were more vulnerable to being bullied online than those aged 8-12. However, parents worried
20　less about the older group using a tablet.

David Emm, senior security researcher at Kaspersky Lab said parents were not often as aware of the dangers of using the Internet on tablets and smartphones as they were with PCs.

"When children use mobile devices to access the web, they are using
25　the same Internet, with the same risks," he said.

"There is a common misconception that smartphones and tablets don't need the same level of protection as a PC.

"But with such a high percentage of parents not having a clear view of their children's online activity, this way of thinking needs to change."

Unmonitored losses

30　Apple's iPhone and iPad have restrictions, or parental controls, that can be set using a passcode.

Access to certain apps or websites can be blocked completely or restricted to age appropriate content.

Restricted profile accounts can also be set up on Android smartphones and tablets.

Over 50% of parents who took part in the BBC poll said they had set up parental controls and filters on their tablets but only 40% said they had done the same on their children's smartphones.

Kapersky Lab's own survey revealed that 18% of parents had lost money or data from their own phone or tablet because their children had been using it unmonitored.

In-app purchases made by children when playing games on their parents' phones are often cited as a reason for money being spent unwittingly.

Apple was recently told to refund $32.5 million (£19.8 million) to parents whose children had made purchases without their parents' consent.

Adults were also being warned to stay safe online as Microsoft released its annual online consumer safety research.

It showed that 5% of consumers in the UK had fallen victim to a phishing attack — losing on average £100. Meanwhile, 3% said they had suffered identity theft which had ended up costing them £100.

The software giant recommended that users set PINs for their mobile phones and strong passwords for online accounts.

【Feb 11, 2013 | BBC】

BACKGROUND OF THE NEWS STORY

　今回はイギリス発信のニュースだが、子供とスマホをめぐるトラブルは、全世界共通の悩みだ。「スマホ依存症」や「ネット炎上」といった言葉が巷にあふれ、LINEを連絡手段にした傷害致死事件も起きた。スマートフォンの普及に伴い、絵本やパズル、歌など乳幼児向けのアプリも増え、乳児に1人で遊ばせるといったスマホ依存低年齢化傾向もみられる。日本小児科医会は、乳幼児にスマートフォンを渡して遊ばせる行為は、子供の健全な発育を妨げる恐れがあると警告を発している。スマートフォンの画面にタッチするだけでは決して得ることのできない、直接体験による刺激や、家族や友人との実際のふれあいを通じて、人は五感を研ぎ澄ましていくということを改めて確認したい。

Comprehension Check

■ *True or False*

英文を日本語にし、ニュースの内容に合っていればT（True）、間違っていればF（False）に〇をつけましょう。

1. Most parents are so strict that they are always checking how their kids use their smartphones or tablets.
   (T ／ F)

2. Smartphones and tablets do not need the same level of protection as PCs.
   (T ／ F)

3. Kids are flexible so they are immune from encountering problems online.
   (T ／ F)

■ *Multiple Choice*

適切なものを（A）（B）（C）（D）より選びましょう。

1. According to the _____ , many parents let their kid use tablets or smartphones without presence of them.
   (A) teachers   (B) parents   (C) survey   (D) experts

2. In order to prevent children from accessing _____ website, parents can set restrictions using a passcode.
   (A) vulnerable   (B) inappropriate   (C) educational   (D) annual

3. In some cases, parents _____ pay for applications their kids bought on line.
   (A) especially   (B) truly   (C) unknowingly   (D) severely

Practical Tips

- vulnerableは、「負傷する」という意味のラテン語源の形容詞で「傷つきやすい」「影響を受けやすい」「無防備な」という意味です。肉体的な弱さにも精神的な脆さにも使えます。反対はinvulnerable。物が壊れやすいという場合は、fragileを使います。配達物にfragileとあったら「割れ物注意」です。
- identity theftは「個人情報の盗難／窃盗」です。identityは「本人であること」「身元」という意味で、theftは「窃盗（罪）」です。theftは簡単にstealingでもOKです。thiefは「窃盗を働く人、泥棒」です。武器を使う強盗犯人＝robber（強盗罪はrobbery）と異なり、コッソリ盗むという感じですね。

Grammar Build-up

Incomplete Sentence

適切なものを (A) (B) (C) (D) より選び、文法上正しい英文を完成させましょう。

1. I ran _____ one of my high school classmates for the first time in 10 years.
   (A) out of   (B) about   (C) around   (D) into

2. Jack picked out targets of _____ one after another.
   (A) bully   (B) bullies   (C) bullying   (D) bullied

3. The bank urged him that he _____ his password once in a while.
   (A) changes   (B) change   (C) changed   (D) will change

Rearrange in the Correct Order

順番を並べ替えて、意味の通る英文にしてください。（最初の文字は大文字に変更してください。）また、それを日本語にしましょう。

1. must ／ of ／ stock ／ be ／ of ／ dangers ／ trading ／ aware ／ you

   英文：_____

   訳：_____

2. touch ／ is ／ reality ／ with ／ celebrity ／ out ／ the ／ of

   英文：_____

   訳：_____

3. biannually ／ are ／ company ／ bonus ／ employees ／ given ／ their

   英文：_____

   訳：_____

English-Japanese translation

次の英文の動詞を○で囲み、日本語にしましょう。

1. Only about 20% of people surveyed say they support the newly-announced polity.

   _____

2. Japanese males in certain age group are said to be not immune to rubella because regular vaccinations for boys were not required.

   _____

3. If you were asked your PIN number by someone, you have to be watchful because it might be some sort of ID theft.

   _____

Further Study

◻ Make sentences using the following words

下の英単語の、ニュース本文の中で使われている品詞と意味を辞書で調べて書き、その単語が入った8ワード以上のオリジナルセンテンスを作りましょう。

	品詞	意味	その他の品詞や意味
1. device	_____	_____	_____
2. purchase	_____	_____	_____
3. commission	_____	_____	_____

◻ Speak up about the News

以下の会話を聴き、空欄を埋めましょう。

Newcy: (　　　) (　　　) (　　　)? My little sister was asking my parents to buy her a smartphone this morning! I'm so (　　　)!

Jijio: (　　　) (　　　)? My little brother got one and he said it's (　　　) for him because he gets (　　　) about his friends, and my parents say that it's easy for them to know his (　　　).

Newcy: But my sister is only 9 years old! She won't know how to use it properly yet.

Jijio: Oh, I see. I (　　　) what age kids should be allowed to have smartphones. I got mine when I turned 18.

Newcy: Well, I got mine when I was 15 but my parents always check on how I'm using it. They are very strict (　　　) when I'm using social networking sites. My mom even (　　　) her own account on Facebook to check on me!

◻ Voice your Opinion

How old were you when you began using your own mobile phone? How old do you think kids should be allowed to have a smartphone? Why?

教育・一般③

第11章：コピペにレッドカード

単語数：639
難度 ★☆☆

Before Reading

　STAP細胞問題を契機に、学術界を中心にコピペ（copy and paste）対策に注目が集まっている。コピペは今に始まった問題ではないが、インターネットの普及が昨今の状況をより複雑にしていることは間違いない。正しい著作権の知識を身につけたい。

■ Basic Vocabulary Building

英語に合う日本語を選びましょう。

1. credit　　　　　　　　a. 違法行為
2. tempting　　　　　　　b. 〜に続いて
3. misconduct　　　　　　c. 疑念
4. in the wake of　　　　d. 魅力的な
5. suspicion　　　　　　 e. 功績とする

■ Advanced Vocabulary Building

英語に合う日本語を選びましょう。

1. alteration　　　　　　a. 議論のある
2. breach　　　　　　　　b. 改ざん
3. contentious　　　　　 c. 盗作
4. plagiarism　　　　　　d. ねつ造
5. fabrication　　　　　 e. 違反

■ Pronunciation Training

アクセントのある母音に○をつけ、発音に注意して5回声に出して読んでみましょう。

1. volume　　2. theses　　3. specific　　4. preventative　　5. acquisition

71

Let's Read

Japanese universities rush to tackle cheating in wake of STAP cell controversy

Universities across Japan are moving quickly to expand ethics instruction for students as irregularities in papers on stimulus-triggered acquisition of pluripotency (STAP) cells continue to make headlines. Many schools are also adopting software to check student papers for
5 copy-and-paste plagiarism.

"What's most important is to teach students that cheating does them no good," one expert told the Mainichi about the renewed efforts to keep students honest.

One institution with a long history of ethics instruction is Waseda
10 University, the alma mater of Haruko Obokata, Riken institute researcher and lead author on the contentious STAP cell papers. Every student entering the school since 1997 — undergrad or graduate — has had to take an information ethics class that covers the copy-and-paste problem. In 2008, Waseda also began a course in research ethics, and in 2012
15 became the first Japanese university to start using the plagiarism-detecting software iThenticate to check student essays and theses.

And yet, suspicions arose recently that Obokata copied one part of her doctoral thesis from a U.S. research website. Waseda is now awaiting the final report of an internal investigative committee on the issue, and will
20 consider new policies to prevent further instances of plagiarism.

Nagoya University President Michinari Hamaguchi is trying to bring home the message that plagiarism is a shameful act. Hamaguchi used his speech at an April 5 graduate school entrance ceremony to tell the new students, "To copy and paste is to throw away your pride and self-respect
25 as scientists. Altering data, too, makes fools of most people." Nagoya University is also now considering a trial implementation of the iThenticate system.

Kinki University in Osaka Prefecture, meanwhile, issued a reminder to its researchers warning against misconduct in both academic papers and
30 research expense claims. The school had earlier pondered a research ethics program for its teaching staff, but "must now draw up new policies to combat copy-and-paste plagiarism among all students, whether in the humanities or the sciences. We are moving to consider the specifics of these policies," according to the university's public relations department.
35 Doshisha University in Kyoto Prefecture set research ethics standards

NOTES

in wake of 〜に続いて（通例 in the wake of 〜）

STAP 刺激惹起性多能性獲得 (stimulus-triggered acquisition of pluripotency)

controversy 論争

ethics 倫理

irregularity 不正行為、規則違反

make headlines 新聞（など）に大きく取りあげられる

plagiarism 盗作、盗用

institution （公共）機関

alma mater 母校、出身校

institute （研究目的の）機関

contentious 議論のある

undergrad 大学生

graduate 大学院生

thesis 論文（複数形は theses）

arise 生じる

doctoral 博士号の

bring home 痛感させる

make fools of 〜 馬鹿にする（= make a fool of 〜）

reminder 注意喚起文書

misconduct 違法行為

ponder じっくり考える

humanities and sciences 文系と理系

for its teaching staff in 2005, and also has a training program to prevent ethical breaches. The recent controversy over Obokata and the STAP cell papers, however, has prompted the school to take another look at rules for students against "information fabrication, alteration and plagiarism" in papers as well.

Tokyo's Seikei University, meanwhile, is planning an assembly for science majors and graduate students on research ethics. The university's Faculty of Science and Technology already has a research ethics course, but "we want to make undergraduates more aware of the issue from now on," a Seikei spokesperson said.

To prevent violations of academic ethical standards, the vast majority of universities direct their students to always credit their sources and steer clear of copying other people's work. With computers now commonplace, however, copying and pasting is now a simple and potentially tempting reality.

This has led to the popularity of software like iThenticate that checks papers for text copied from other sources. Rikkyo University, where all teaching staff began using a plagiarism detection program last year, told the Mainichi that adopting the software "was necessary because of the sheer volume of student reports that need to be checked quickly."

A company that developed similar software commented, "We used to get two or three inquiries from universities a day, but since the recent (Obokata) controversy we've seen three times that."

Akira Tachi, a professor of education at J.F. Oberlin University in Tokyo, told the Mainichi, "The ease of copying and pasting has made committing academic misconduct easier as well, and universities are being called upon to implement a range of preventative policies. However, the best preventive policy is to let students know that cheating will do them no good in the end."

【April 12, 2014 | Mainichi Japan】

Comprehension Check

◻ *True or False*

英文を日本語にし、ニュースの内容に合っていればT（True）、間違っていればF（False）に○をつけましょう。

1. After the STAP cell scandal, universities across Japan reacted quickly against copy-and-paste cheating.
   _____ (T ／ F)

2. Meiji University is the first university to use iThenticate to check students' essays and theses for plagiarism.
   _____ (T ／ F)

3. The news about the controversial STAP cells got a lot of media coverage.
   _____ (T ／ F)

◻ *Multiple Choice*

適切なものを（A）（B）（C）（D）より選びましょう。

1. What does the following statement refer to: a piece of writing that has been copied from someone else and is presented as being your own work?
   (A) vandalism   (B) plagiarism   (C) fascism   (D) commercialism

2. Which university is the lead researcher and author of STAP cell research graduate from?
   (A) Kinki University   (B) Doshisha University
   (C) Rikkyo University   (D) Waseda University

3. According to the article, what makes it easier to copy and paste other people's work?
   (A) borrowing books in libraries   (B) lenient teachers
   (C) easy access to computers   (D) hectic research schedule

Practical Tips

- 見出しに使われている in the wake of は「～の後に続いて」です。シンプルに following や after としてもOKですが、ニュース英語でよく使われる表現です。wake は船の通った後を表す「航跡」という意味です。
- thesis「論文」を複数形にすると theses となります。発音は【θíːsiːz】となることに注意しましょう。sis で終わる語は他に、analysis「分析」、crisis「危機」、axis「軸」などで、複数形は analyses, crises, axes となります。
- 本文には institute と institution の両方が出ています。institute は学術や芸術などのための協会や研究所に使い、institution は教育、社会、慈善、宗教などの活動のための機関に使います。

Grammar Build-up

Incomplete Sentence

適切なものを (A) (B) (C) (D) より選び、文法上正しい英文を完成させましょう。

1. We had our batch reunion in our _____ .
   (A) alma mater (B) coup d'etat (C) status quo (D) vice versa

2. Making fools of people might be regarded as _____ .
   (A) eulogy (B) flattery (C) bullying (D) tribute

3. Using a smartphone in public transportations has now become a _____ .
   (A) common   (B) commonplace
   (C) commoner   (D) common place

Rearrange in the Correct Order

順番を並べ替えて、意味の通る英文にしてください。（最初の文字は大文字に変更してください。）また、それを日本語にしましょう。

1. home / please / make / at / yourself

   英文：_____

   訳：_____

2. excuse / she / late / an / being / fabricated / for

   英文：_____

   訳：_____

3. after / a date / pondering / her / for / he / asked

   英文：_____

   訳：_____

English-Japanese translation

次の英文の動詞を○で囲み、日本語にしましょう。

1. Prof. Yamanaka was awarded the Nobel Prize for his research on iPS cells.

2. Many people pin their hope on the successful creation of regenerative medicines.

3. Once credited as "Japan's Beethoven," he made an apology for his ghostwriting scandal in the end.

Further Study

Make sentences using the following words

下の英単語の、ニュース本文の中で使われている品詞と意味を辞書で調べて書き、その単語が入った8ワード以上のオリジナルセンテンスを作りましょう。

	品詞	意味	その他の品詞や意味
1. institute	_____	_____	_____
2. institution	_____	_____	_____
3. humanity	_____	_____	_____

Speak up about the News

以下の会話を聴き、空欄を埋めましょう。

Jijio: The submission of our (　　　　) will be at the end of this month. It took me (　　　　) (　　　　) a month to finish half of mine. How are you doing with yours?

Newcy: Oh, that... yeah.... ummm. I haven't finished even half of it. But I will finish it before the (　　　　). A lot of information is (　　　　) through online resources.

Jijio: You must be extra (　　　　) in referring to them. Information (　　　　) on the Internet is not always (　　　　). Furthermore, (　　　　) (　　　　) (　　　　) other people's work is never a good thing. You don't want to be accused of (　　　　). You would be (　　　　) (　　　　) of the school.

Newcy: Don't worry. I mean I worked on a (　　　　) thesis last year and the paper I am working on is like a (　　　　) type. That's why I said I can still do it, (　　　　) the limited time. I do not like walking a (　　　　).

Voice your Opinion

Some people have reservations when it comes to regenerative medicine due to ethical reasons. What is your opinion about regenerative medicine?

第12章：近大養殖マグロレストラン

単語数：673
難度 ★☆☆

Before Reading

　1970年に養殖マグロの研究を開始した近畿大学水産研究所。数々の苦労の末に2002年に世界で初めて人工ふ化した稚魚から育てる完全養殖に成功した。大阪店も、第二号店の銀座店も盛況だ。

Basic Vocabulary Building

英語に合う日本語を選びましょう。

1. contribute
2. prominent
3. convey
4. available
5. species

a. 伝える
b. 種
c. 卓越した
d. 貢献する
e. 入手できる

Advanced Vocabulary Building

英語に合う日本語を選びましょう。

1. hazardous
2. conventional
3. palate
4. stipulate
5. depletion

a. 枯渇
b. 味覚
c. 危険な
d. 規定する
e. 従来の

Pronunciation Training

アクセントのある母音に○をつけ、発音に注意して5回声に出して読んでみましょう。

1. laboratory　2. superior　3. contribute　4. gourmet　5. cultivate

Let's Read

'Kindai' bluefin tuna set to delight taste buds in Osaka

Osaka — On a recent spring day at the Knowledge Capital complex in the Grand Front Osaka redeveloped area, workers could be seen rushing about to complete preparations for the opening of the Fisheries Laboratory of Kinki University.

5 What sounds like a place of scientific research is actually a new restaurant scheduled to have its grand opening on April 26 in the Umekita district, located north of JR Osaka Station.

Fisheries Laboratory of Kinki University will specialize in "Kindai" tuna, bluefin tuna that are 100 percent farmed from bluefin roe at Kinki 10 University.

The university succeeded in farming bluefin from farmed fish eggs about 10 years ago. Fisheries Laboratory of Kinki University will be the first restaurant in Japan to specialize in serving 100 percent farmed bluefin tuna in Japan.

15 Kindai tuna may be new to Japanese palates, but the fish are well-known among sushi and sashimi lovers in the United States. In 2007, Tetsuya Sakagami, who operates a trading house in Los Angeles, began to import the university's bluefin and promoted it to chefs of first-class restaurants in New York. As a result, Kindai tuna has spread to restaurants 20 throughout the United States.

"I wanted to convey (to the American people) that Japan is contributing to the protection of marine resources with its prominent fish farming techniques," Sakagami said.

The fish have been widely accepted in the United States, where 25 gourmets usually prefer farmed fish to naturally grown ones due to possible contamination by hazardous materials, such as mercury, in fish caught in the wild.

Back home in February, the organizers of the Fisheries Laboratory of Kinki University held a Kindai tuna tasting party in Osaka. Students and 30 other maguro (tuna) lovers ate sashimi and menchi-katsu (deep-fried minced meat) and were surprised by the delicious taste of the Kindai tuna.

"It has plenty of fat even in the lean portions," said one of the participants.

35 "The taste is rich," added another.

Some of the participants said the taste of the Kindai tuna was superior

---

NOTES

bluefin tuna クロマグロ
taste bud 味蕾(みらい)
Grand Front Osaka redeveloped area グランドフロント大阪再開発地域
rush about 急いで飛び回る
district 地域
specialize in ～を専門にする
roe 魚卵

palate 味覚、嗜好

trading house 貿易商社

convey 伝える
contribute 貢献する
prominent 卓越した

gourmet 美食家、食通
contamination 汚染
hazardous 危険な
material 物質
mercury 水銀

lean portion 脂肪分の少ない、赤みの部位
participant 参加者

superior まさった

to tuna caught in the ocean.

Despite the glowing taste tests, Kinki University, based in Higashi-Osaka city in Osaka Prefecture, is still facing difficulties in popularizing its tuna among Japanese consumers.

One problem is price.

Conventional tuna farming uses bluefin fry caught in their natural environment. But Kindai tuna are raised from fry that are cultivated on the fish farm. As a result, prices of 100 percent farmed tuna are 20 to 30 percent higher than those of the conventional farmed fish.

Another hurdle is the Japanese "sense of value," where in the case of fish, naturally grown ones are deemed the best.

To overcome the problem, the university has been publicizing the "environmentally friendly aspect" of its farmed bluefin tuna. The decision is based on the university's success of spreading Kindai tuna in the United States.

The restaurant will be located in the soon-to-open Knowledge Capital, a core facility of the Grand Front Osaka redeveloped area in the Umekita district. Knowledge Capital will be set up to promote exchanges among researchers of companies and universities in hopes of developing advanced technologies and goods.

Fisheries Laboratory of Kinki University plans to have tablet computers available to diners at the restaurant that will show how the university cultivates its bluefin.

The university hopes that if customers eat Kindai tuna while thinking about the problems of marine resources, they will come to prefer the tuna.

In developing menus for the restaurant, the university was assisted by the Suntory group, which operates many restaurants.

Japan is the largest consumer of tuna in the world, consuming about 80 percent of the bluefin species caught across the globe.

Catches of bluefin tuna are now under restrictions due to fear of depletion. In 2011, a total of 40,700 tons of bluefin tuna was supplied in Japan. Of that, more than half was caught in the Pacific Ocean.

Starting in 2011, international regulations stipulate that catches of Pacific bluefin tuna will be reduced from the annual average of the period from 2002 to 2004.

【April 24, 2013 | By Aki Sato — Asahi Shimbun】

NOTES

despite にもかかわらず
glowing 輝かしい
popularize 普及させる

conventional 従来の
fry 稚魚、小魚
cultivate 養殖する

deem みなす

available 入手できる
diner 食事をする人
cultivate 養殖する

species 種
catch 漁獲
depletion 枯渇

stipulate 規定する

Comprehension Check

True or False

英文を日本語にし、ニュースの内容に合っていればT（True）、間違っていればF（False）に〇をつけましょう。

1. The new restaurant bears a name which does not sound like an eating establishment.

   (T／F)

2. Kindai tuna is famous across the United States because one Japanese businessman recommended it to high-end restaurants there.

   (T／F)

3. People place their hopes on Kindai tuna because bluefin tuna fishing in the wild is now being banned all together.

   (T／F)

Multiple Choice

適切なものを（A）（B）（C）（D）より選びましょう。

1. The university successfully farmed bluefin tuna from cultivated fish eggs about a _____ ago.
   (A) month   (B) year   (C) century   (D) decade

2. Some foodie people in the United States believe that farmed fish is _____ than fish caught in the ocean.
   (A) more hazardous   (B) bigger   (C) more delicious   (D) safer

3. Kindai University has played up bluefin tuna farming as _____ approach.
   (A) an eco-friendly   (B) a logical
   (C) a userfriendly   (D) a cost-effective

Practical Tips

- farmというと「農場」をイメージする人が多いと思いますが、「（魚などの）養殖場」にも使います。また「文化」の意味でお馴染みのcultureにも「養殖、培養」の意味があります。本文では、cultivateも「養殖する」の意味で使われていますね。「水産養殖」にはaquacultureも使えます。
- レストランなどに食事に来る客はdinerです。dineは「食事をする」という動詞で、dine and wine = wine and dineは「おおいにもてなす、接待する」です。dinerは「食堂車」という意味もあります。「お客」を表す英語は、一般的にはcustomer、「買い物客」にはshopper、「訪問客」はvisitor、「旅行者」はtourist、パーティやホテルではguestです。それに加えて、弁護士など専門家に相談を求める「顧客」clientなどは覚えておきましょう。

Grammar Build-up

Incomplete Sentence

適切なものを（A）（B）（C）（D）より選び、文法上正しい英文を完成させましょう。

1. Some people prefer camping _____ staying in hotels.
   (A) than   (B) to   (C) and   (D) with

2. He failed the exam _____ his efforts in hitting the books all night.
   (A) in spite   (B) instead of   (C) despite   (D) regardless

3. Japanese people eat more tuna than people in _____ country in the world.
   (A) any more   (B) no other   (C) any other   (D) every other

Rearrange in the Correct Order

順番を並べ替えて、意味の通る英文にしてください。（最初の文字は大文字に変更してください。）また、それを日本語にしましょう。

1. species ／ creatures ／ on ／ endangered ／ list ／ are ／ many ／ the ／ of

   英文：＿＿＿＿＿＿＿＿＿＿＿＿＿＿＿＿＿＿＿＿＿＿＿＿＿＿＿＿
   訳：＿＿＿＿＿＿＿＿＿＿＿＿＿＿＿＿＿＿＿＿＿＿＿＿＿＿＿＿

2. metals ／ to ／ hazardous ／ heavy ／ are ／ health

   英文：＿＿＿＿＿＿＿＿＿＿＿＿＿＿＿＿＿＿＿＿＿＿＿＿＿＿＿＿
   訳：＿＿＿＿＿＿＿＿＿＿＿＿＿＿＿＿＿＿＿＿＿＿＿＿＿＿＿＿

3. deemed ／ I ／ be ／ a ／ to ／ genius ／ him

   英文：＿＿＿＿＿＿＿＿＿＿＿＿＿＿＿＿＿＿＿＿＿＿＿＿＿＿＿＿
   訳：＿＿＿＿＿＿＿＿＿＿＿＿＿＿＿＿＿＿＿＿＿＿＿＿＿＿＿＿

English-Japanese translation

次の英文の動詞を○で囲み、日本語にしましょう。

1. The Minamata Convention was adopted to regulate the use and trade of mercury.

2. Correcting discrepancies in the value of individual votes among electoral districts is important.

3. Carbon dioxide is known as the culprit in the depletion of the ozone layer.

Further Study

■ Make sentences using the following words

下の英単語の、ニュース本文の中で使われている品詞と意味を辞書で調べて書き、その単語が入った8ワード以上のオリジナルセンテンスを作りましょう。

		品詞	意味	その他の品詞や意味
1.	specialize	___	___	___
2.	lean	___	___	___
3.	diner	___	___	___

■ Speak up about the News

以下の会話を聴き、空欄を埋めましょう。

Jijio: My brother received his first (　　　) yesterday, so he took the (　　　) family to a restaurant.

Newcy: Oh, your brother is so (　　　)! How was the restaurant?

Jijio: We went to the (　　　) Kindai tuna restaurant. (　　　), I can't tell the (　　　) between 100% farmed tuna and tuna from the wild, but it was good!

Newcy: Oh (　　　) (　　　)! I've always wanted to (　　　) it. Tell me more about it.

Jijio: Oh, you won't believe it but the dishes were served with (　　　) for the fish. They say it's to (　　　) its taste, and I must agree. It was really good.

■ English Composition

次の日本語を英語にしましょう。

1. 新しくオープンしたそのレストランはイタリア料理専門店だ。
   specialize in を使って

2. そのアプリはインターネットで無料で手に入れることが出来る。
   available を使って

3. その会議の参加者数は予想を超えた。
   participant を使って

海外ニュース③

第13章：ローマ法王、タイム誌の「今年の人」に

単語数：588
難度 ★★★

Before Reading

官僚主義やスキャンダルに揺れるバチカン。フランシスコ法王は、社会的弱者に寄り添い、特権や虚飾を嫌い、中絶や同性愛にも関心を向けるなど、今までの法王とは一風変わったスタイルで注目が集まっている。

Basic Vocabulary Building

英語に合う日本語を選びましょう。

1. honor
2. obsession
3. predecessor
4. proclaim
5. fame

a. 公言する
b. 前任者
c. 名声
d. 妄想
e. 栄誉

Advanced Vocabulary Building

英語に合う日本語を選びましょう。

1. implicitly
2. frugality
3. penchant
4. abdicate
5. downtrodden

a. 王位などを捨てる
b. 踏みにじられた
c. 暗に
d. 趣味、好み
e. 倹約

Pronunciation Training

アクセントのある母音に〇をつけ、発音に注意して5回声に出して読んでみましょう。

1. disillusioned   2. archbishop   3. advocacy   4. spacious   5. hastily

Let's Read

Pope Francis named *Time*'s Person of the Year

Time magazine named Pope Francis its Person of the Year on Wednesday, crediting him with shifting the message of the Catholic Church while capturing the imagination of millions of people who had become disillusioned with the Vatican.

This is the third time the magazine has chosen a pope as its Person of the Year. *Time* gave that honor to Pope John Paul II in 1994 and to Pope John XXIII in 1963.

The Argentine pontiff — who, as archbishop of Buenos Aires was known as the slum cardinal for his visits to the poor and penchant for subway travel — beat former U.S. National Security Agency contractor Edward Snowden and gay rights activist Edith Windsor for the award.

Other finalists included Syrian President Bashar al-Assad and U.S. Senator Ted Cruz from Texas.

"What makes this Pope so important is the speed with which he has captured the imaginations of millions who had given up on hoping for the church at all," *Time* said in its cover story.

"In a matter of months, Francis has elevated the healing mission of the church — the church as servant and comforter of hurting people in an often harsh world — above the doctrinal police work so important to his recent predecessors."

Time said the final selection was made by its editors, who had considered suggestions from the magazine's more than 2 million Twitter followers.

Vatican spokesman Father Federico Lombardi said Pope Francis, the first non-European pope in 1,300 years, the first from Latin America and the first Jesuit, was not seeking fame.

"It is a positive sign that one of the most prestigious recognitions by the international media has been given to a person who proclaims to the world spiritual, religious and moral values and speaks out forcefully in favor of peace and greater justice," Lombardi said in a statement.

"If this attracts men and women and gives them hope, the Pope is happy. If this choice of 'Person of the Year' means that many have understood this message, even implicitly, he is certainly glad."

In September, Francis gave a groundbreaking and frank interview, in which he said the Vatican must shake off an obsession with teachings on abortion, contraception and homosexuality, and become more merciful.

And in July, Francis told reporters he was not in a position to judge homosexuals who are of good will and in search of God, marking a break from his predecessor, Benedict, who said homosexuality was an intrinsic disorder.

Francis replaced Benedict in March after he abdicated.

The new pope's style is characterized by frugality. He shunned the spacious papal apartment in the Vatican's Apostolic Palace to live in a small suite in a Vatican guest house, and he prefers a Ford Focus to the traditional pope's Mercedes.

A champion of the downtrodden, he visited the island of Lampedusa in southern Italy in July to pay tribute to hundreds of migrants who had died crossing the sea from North Africa.

With the Catholic Church marred in recent years by sex abuse scandals, Francis formed a team of experts Thursday to consider ways to improve the screening of priests, to protect minors to help victims.

Still, Barbara Blaine, president of the Survivors Network of those Abused by Priests (SNAP), a victim advocacy group, said in a statement Wednesday that more action was needed.

"After nine months of essentially ignoring the church's most severe crisis, (Pope Francis) hastily announced last week that he'll appoint an abuse study panel," Blaine said. "He has not, however, made a single child safer."

【Dec, 11, 2013 | By Elizabeth Dilts ― Reuters】

NOTES

shake off 取り除く
obsession (頭から離れない) 妄想
abortion 中絶
contraception 避妊
homosexuality 同性愛
merciful 慈悲深い
intrinsic 固有の
disorder 障害
replace 後継者となる
abdicate (王位等を) 放棄する
frugality 倹約
shun 避ける
spacious 広々とした
papal 法王の
champion 擁護者
downtrodden 踏みにじられた
pay tribute 敬意を表する
migrants 移民
sex abuse 性的虐待
screening 適性審査
priest 司祭
minor 未成年者
victim 犠牲者
advocacy 擁護
hastily 急いで

BACKGROUND OF THE NEWS STORY

1923年創刊の米国ニュース雑誌『タイム』は2013年のPerson of the Yearにフランシスコ法王を選んだ。最終選考リスト10人の中には、米国家安全保障局の秘密を暴露したエドワード・スノーデン氏、同性愛者の権利擁護活動家のエディス・ウィンザー氏、シリアのアサド大統領らがいた。

12億人の信者と巨大な富と重い歴史を担うローマ法王は、バチカンの官僚主義、性的虐待スキャンダル、マネーロンダリングと腐敗、司祭の高齢化など数々の問題を抱えている。フランシスコ法王は就任以降、「小さいことにこだわる規則」にこだわることで中絶、同性愛、離婚といった微妙な問題への対応で教義を押しつけることのないよう求めている。特権や虚飾を嫌い、宮殿ではなく他の司祭たちと宿舎に住み、ベンツを古いフォードに変え、赤い靴や赤い法衣を、黒い靴、白い衣にし、金の十字架ではなく鉄の十字架を下げている。

Comprehension Check

◘ *True or False*

英文を日本語にし、ニュースの内容に合っていればT（True）、間違っていればF（False）に〇をつけましょう。

1. Pope Benedict is the first pontiff from Latin America.
   _____ (T ／ F)

2. Pope Francis gave a statement in a frank interview that the church should be more open to the discussion of reproductive health issues.
   _____ (T ／ F)

3. Roman Catholic Church's reputation has been damaged by a series of scandals including child sexual abuse cases by priests.
   _____ (T ／ F)

◘ *Multiple Choice*

適切なものを（A）（B）（C）（D）より選びましょう。

1. Pope Francis is remarkably different from his _____ on several issues such as showing understanding for homosexuality.
   (A) successors (B) ancestors (C) predecessors (D) followers

2. What is the issue that Ms. Barbara Blaine is accusing Pope Francis of ignoring?
   (A) sexual abuse scandals   (B) money laundering scandal
   (C) homosexuality scandal   (D) human trafficking scandal

3. Who is the 2nd pope to be awarded "Person of the Year" from *Time* magazine?
   (A) Pope Paul VI   (B) Pope John Paul II
   (C) Pope Francis   (D) Pope Benedict XVI

Practical Tips

- ローマカトリック関連の単語は馴染みが薄いかもしれません。バチカンのトップは「法王」popeもしくはpontiffです。法王はcardinal「枢機卿」の中から、conclaveと呼ばれる法王選挙秘密会議で選出されます。deacon「助祭」、priest「司祭」、bishop「司教」、archbishop「大司教」そして、cardinalの順に位が高くなります。
- abortion「中絶」の問題は、アメリカ大統領選挙の時にも争点の一つです。その際よく耳にする表現は、pro-life（生命を尊重）→中絶合法化反対と、それに対して、pro-choice（産む産まない選択を尊重）→中絶合法化賛成です。これはIncomplete Sentence 3問目のヒントです。

Grammar Build-up

Incomplete Sentence

適切なものを (A) (B) (C) (D) より選び、文法上正しい英文を完成させましょう。

1. The Japanese government officials visited Yasukuni Shrine in order to pay _____ to the war dead.
   (A) tax (B) pension (C) benefit (D) tribute

2. 3-D printer technology is _____ groundbreaking that it can make a prosthetic limb only for about 100 dollars.
   (A) very (B) so (C) too (D) far

3. GOP regards itself as the _____-life and pro-family party.
   (A) pro (B) post (C) pre (D) anti

Rearrange in the Correct Order

順番を並べ替えて、意味の通る英文にしてください。(最初の文字は大文字に変更してください。) また、それを日本語にしましょう。

1. overlooked ／ often ／ abuse ／ is ／ child
   英文：＿＿＿＿＿＿＿＿＿＿＿＿＿＿＿＿＿＿＿
   訳：＿＿＿＿＿＿＿＿＿＿＿＿＿＿＿＿＿＿＿

2. Edward Snowden ／ calls ／ US ／ whistle-blower ／ a
   英文：＿＿＿＿＿＿＿＿＿＿＿＿＿＿＿＿＿＿＿
   訳：＿＿＿＿＿＿＿＿＿＿＿＿＿＿＿＿＿＿＿

3. elected ／ cardinals ／ Pope ／ from ／ is
   英文：＿＿＿＿＿＿＿＿＿＿＿＿＿＿＿＿＿＿＿
   訳：＿＿＿＿＿＿＿＿＿＿＿＿＿＿＿＿＿＿＿

English-Japanese translation

次の英文の動詞を○で囲み、日本語にしましょう。

1. Ten Japanese were captured and killed in the terrorist crisis in Algeria.

2. Edward VIII is famous for abdicating his throne to marry a woman he loves.

3. Vatican watchers say his efforts to help the poor, together with his humble manner and sense of humor, have made him popular.

Further Study

■ Make sentences using the following words

下の英単語の、ニュース本文の中で使われている品詞と意味を辞書で調べて書き、その単語が入った8ワード以上のオリジナルセンテンスを作りましょう。

	品詞	意味	その他の品詞や意味
1. credit	_____	_____	_____
2. minor	_____	_____	_____
3. abuse	_____	_____	_____

■ Speak up about the News

以下の会話を聴き、空欄を埋めましょう。

Newcy: What are you reading?

Jijio: I'm reading *Time* magazine. I don't read it (   ), but I (   ) one today because I thought the cover picture was (   ).

Newcy: Who's on the cover? Let me see.... Oh, it's Pope Francis. He's very popular (   ) (   ) to Catholics, (   ) (   ) to non-Catholics.

Jijio: How does *Time* choose the "Person of the Year"?

Newcy: *Time* gives the (   ) annually to a person, group, idea or object that most (   ) the news and people's lives, (   ) (   ) (   ) (   ) (   ).

■ Voice your Opinion

What ability do you think is essential for a religious leader to lead his/her organization?

社会問題③

第14章：Jリーグ初の無観客試合

単語数：528
難度 ★★☆

Before Reading

浦和レッズのサポーター席に入るゲートに日章旗と共に掲げられた問題の横断幕。Jリーグ22年の歴史の中で、最も重い無観客試合の処分となった。「差別撲滅宣言」を読み上げた後、通常は声援で湧くさいたまスタジアムにはボールを蹴る音のみが響いた。

Basic Vocabulary Building

英語に合う日本語を選びましょう。

1. ban
2. perceive
3. constitute
4. indefinitely
5. deem

a. 構成する
b. 知覚する
c. 永遠に
d. みなす
e. 禁止する

Advanced Vocabulary Building

英語に合う日本語を選びましょう。

1. censure
2. taunt
3. repercussion
4. sanction
5. offense

a. なじる、あざける
b. 違反、反則
c. 制裁措置を取る
d. 余波
e. 非難する

Pronunciation Training

アクセントのある母音に○をつけ、発音に注意して5回声に出して読んでみましょう。

1. average　2. prohibit　3. competition　4. judiciary　5. foreseeable

Let's Read

Soccer: Reds ordered to play behind closed doors for racist banner

Tokyo — The J-League came down hard on Urawa Reds for what it deemed as racist fan behavior on Thursday, ordering the former Asian champions to play an upcoming match behind closed doors.

In the stiffest punishment yet issued by the 20-year-old J-League, Urawa, the best supported club in Japan with an average attendance of more than 37,000 last season, must host their March 23 league game against Shimizu S-Pulse in an empty Saitama Stadium.

Playing at home to Sagan Tosu on March 8, Reds allowed a banner that read, "Japanese Only" to be displayed and did not remove it until after the game. Urawa have fielded an all-Japanese lineup in both matches this season.

Reds have identified and indefinitely banned the fans responsible from all their games. They will also prohibit their supporters from displaying signs and banners of any kind in all competitions for the foreseeable future.

While the fans have told the club they had no racist intentions, that is beside the point, says league chairman Mitsuru Murai, who took over from Kazumi Ohigashi in January.

"There are various ways of determining what constitutes discrimination," Murai said in a statement. "But what is important is not so much why discrimination occurs, but how the victim perceives it and in this case, the acts must be considered nothing short of discriminatory."

"Over the last several days through the media and on the Internet, these acts have had unexpected social repercussions both domestic and abroad, and it is clear that they have damaged the brand of not just the J-League but of the entire Japanese football community."

The J-League's stand against racism even drew a reaction from the government.

"This is for the J-League to decide as organizers and the government should probably refrain from commenting," Chief Cabinet Secretary Yoshihide Suga said. "But the way we see it, the J-League acted with speed to the discriminatory banner not being removed soon enough."

Reds have been sanctioned before for racist behavior by their frenetic supporters, being fined 5 million yen and censured in 2010 when fans taunted foreign players of Vegalta Sendai.

NOTES

come down hard on ～をこっぴどくしかる、強く出る
deem みなす
upcoming もうすぐやってくる、次回の
behind closed doors 観客なしで
cf. a behind-closed-doors game 無観客試合
stiff 厳しい
field 出場させる
lineup 顔ぶれ
identify 確認する、突き止める
indefinitely 無期限に
ban 禁止する
foreseeable 予見できる
intention 意図、目的

determine 決定する、確定する
constitute 構成する
discrimination 差別
perceive 知覚する
nothing short of ～に他ならない
discriminatory 差別的な
repercussion 影響、余波（通例～ s）
entire 丸ごと全部の
stand 立場、態度

refrain from ～を控える
Chief Cabinet Secretary 内閣官房長官
sanction 制裁措置を取る
frenetic 熱狂的な、狂

Murai said past offenses by Urawa fans — and not just those involving racism — were taken into account when the league's judiciary committee decided on the punishment.

"With regards to Urawa Reds, they have had repeated trouble with their supporters in the past and the club have previously been sanctioned for racist behavior by their fans," Murai said.

"While these most recent acts were conducted by a small group of supporters, it is with utmost regret that Urawa Reds — who have been with the J-League since its founding year in 1993 and who ought to be an example for all of Japanese football — allowed an incident like this to happen."

"The league has strongly demanded Urawa Reds to accept this decision with the full weight of responsibility and to make sure it does not happen ever again."

Reds president Keizo Fuchita apologized profusely, admitting the club were slow to act.

"We have to go back to the drawing board and rebuild the club so we can continue to enjoy the support we have," Fuchita said.

【Mar 25, 2014 | KYODO / Mainichi】

NOTES

信的な
fine 罰金を科す
censure 非難する
taunt なじる、あざける
offense 違反、反則
take ~ into account ～を考慮する
judiciary 司法の
committee 委員会
previously 以前に
utmost 最大の
regret 後悔
founding 創設の

profusely 豊富に、過度に

go back to the drawing board 白紙に戻ってやり直す

BACKGROUND OF THE NEWS STORY

　国際サッカー連盟（FIFA）は、ヨーロッパを中心に、選手らによる差別的行為や発言が後を絶たないことから、2013年5月、差別撲滅を決議し、NO RACISM（人種差別反対）キャンペーンを開始した。それを受けて、世界各地の加盟団体は、差別的行為に対する「制裁金」や「無観客試合」などの処分を科す事が求められた。
　浦和レッドダイヤモンズは、1950年に現在の三菱重工業のサッカー部として創設され、Jリーグ設立の1993年当初から加盟をしている10チームの中の1つという歴史を持つチームだ。ホームの埼玉スタジアムで、2014年3月23日に行われた浦和レッズ－清水エスパルス戦は、Jリーグ22年目の歴史の中、初めて無観客で行われた。プレイを盛り上げるサポーターの後押しがないまま、結果は1-1で引き分けた。それは2週間前の対サガン鳥栖戦で浦和サポーターが掲げた「JAPANESE ONLY」という横断幕に対する処分であった。静まり返った巨大スタジアム（63,700人収容の埼玉スタジアム2002）で、選手の声とボールを蹴る音だけが響き、粛々と進められていく異様な試合。思慮を欠いた行為がもたらす結末の重さに、多く人が衝撃を受けた事件となった。

Comprehension Check

▪ True or False

英文を日本語にし、ニュースの内容に合っていればT（True）、間違っていればF（False）に○をつけましょう。

1. The discriminatory banner was put down in the middle of the game.
   _____
   (T ／ F)

2. The club was able to catch the people who put the discriminatory banner up.
   _____
   (T ／ F)

3. Those who were responsible for hoisting the banner said they did it out of discriminatory motive.
   _____
   (T ／ F)

▪ Multiple Choice

適切なものを（A）（B）（C）（D）より選びましょう。

1. Urawa Reds is one of the _____ clubs in J-League history.
   (A) traditional　　(B) punctual　　(C) collective　　(D) drastic

2. The act in question at Saitama Stadium has ruined the _____ of Japanese football.
   (A) presentation　　(B) communication
   (C) image　　(D) performance

3. This is not the first time for the club to be punished because of _____ behavior displayed by some fans.
   (A) capitalism　　(B) optimism　　(C) favoritism　　(D) racism

Practical Tips

- a behind-closed-doors game は「無観客試合」にあたる英語ですが、a game without spectators や、a game with no supporters という表現もありました。spectator はスポーツ観戦や野外イベントの参加者です。同じ観客でもコンサートや観劇の場合は audience が使われます。
- offense, defense というと、スポーツの「攻撃」と「防御」という意味もありますが、本ニュースの中で使われている offense は「罪、反則」です。さて Rearrange in the Correct Order の3問目では、どちらの意味でしょうか。辞書でチェックをしてみましょう。

Grammar Build-up

Incomplete Sentence

適切なものを（A）（B）（C）（D）より選び、文法上正しい英文を完成させましょう。

1. The club says it is going to _____ the team from the scratch.
   (A) retire   (B) restructure   (C) replace   (D) return

2. _____ constitutes good performance in figure skating competition is difficult to judge.
   (A) That   (B) Which   (C) What   (D) Who

3. I hope the _____ boss will be much more considerate.
   (A) up-and-coming   (B) forthcoming
   (C) upcoming   (D) incoming

Rearrange in the Correct Order

順番を並べ替えて、意味の通る英文にしてください。（最初の文字は大文字に変更してください。）また、それを日本語にしましょう。

1. take / customer / you / needs / must / account / into
   英文：_____
   訳：_____

2. nothing / miraculous / was / short / victory / the / of
   英文：_____
   訳：_____

3. took / an / he / statement / offense / as / my
   英文：_____
   訳：_____

English-Japanese translation

次の英文の動詞を○で囲み、日本語にしましょう。

1. The government-sanctioned tax hike is going to be implemented soon.

2. Nobody knows about the "behind-the-scenes" fixer of the meeting.

3. Violators of the law are to face a fine of up to 50,000 yen.

Further Study

◻ *Make sentences using the following words*

下の英単語の、ニュース本文の中で使われている品詞と意味を辞書で調べて書き、その単語が入った8ワード以上のオリジナルセンテンスを作りましょう。

	品詞	意味	その他の品詞や意味
1. stiff	_____	_____	_____
2. refrain	_____	_____	_____
3. regret	_____	_____	_____

◻ *Speak up about the News*

以下の会話を聴き、空欄を埋めましょう。

Jijio: Have you heard about the (　　　　) stadium match that the Urawa Reds had in Saitama Stadium? I can't imagine playing soccer without any (　　　　).

Newcy: Ah, yes. I knew about that. The news said that the stadium was eerily quiet. (　　　　), it was some fans who (　　　　) (　　　　) the banner (　　　　) (　　　　).

Jijio: I think the (　　　　) on the team was a bit (　　　　). Players were just also (　　　　) of the situation. Why do they have to be punished for (　　　　) their fans have done.

Newcy: Some say that the supporters are the (　　　　) player of the team. I think the fans are (　　　　) for soccer teams.

◻ *English Composition*

次の日本語を英語にしましょう。

1. メアリーは、口うるさいお客からの電話をさばくのが上手だ。　　 field を使って

2. 核拡散防止条約は、無期限に延期された。　　 indefinitely を使って

3. その大手銀行の倒産は、国全体に強い影響を与えた。　　 repercussions を使って

編著者
　　渡邉 あをい（わたなべ　あをい）

監修者
　　石井 隆之（いしい　たかゆき）

ニュース英語で世界を拓く

2015 年 2 月 20 日　第 1 版発行
2017 年 3 月 10 日　第 4 版発行

編著者──渡邉 あをい

監修者──石井 隆之

発行者──前田 俊秀

発行所──株式会社三修社
　　　　〒150-0001　東京都渋谷区神宮前 2-2-22
　　　　TEL 03-3405-4511 / FAX 03-3405-4522
　　　　振替 00190-9-72758
　　　　http://www.sanshusha.co.jp/

印刷所──萩原印刷株式会社

Ⓒ 2015 Printed in Japan　ISBN978-4-384-33451-7　C1082
表紙デザイン──岩井デザイン
本文イラスト──浪花まいこ（RHIZOME デザイン事務所）
準拠 CD 録音──一般財団法人 英語教育協議会（ELEC）
準拠 CD 制作──高速録音株式会社
編　　　　集──山本 拓

JCOPY〈出版者著作権管理機構 委託出版物〉

本書の無断複製は著作権法上での例外を除き禁じられています。複製される場合は、そのつど事前に、出版者著作権管理機構（電話 03-3513-6969 FAX 03-3513-6979 e-mail: info@jcopy.or.jp）の許諾を得てください。

教科書準拠 CD 発売
本書の準拠 CD をご希望の方は弊社までお問い合わせください。